McGraw-Hill/Contemporary's

The GED Math Problem Solver

Teacher's Guide, 2nd edition

Myrna Manly

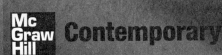

Executive Editor: Linda Kwil
Production Manager: Genevieve Kelley
Marketing Manager: Sean Klunder
Cover Design: Michael E. Kelly

Send all inquiries to:
McGraw-Hill/Contemporary
130 East Randolph Street, Suite 400
Chicago, Illinois 60601

ISBN 0-07-252756-0

Printed in the United States of America.

1 2 3 4 5 6 7 8 9 10 QPD 09 08 07 06 05 04 03

The **McGraw·Hill** Companies

Table of Contents

Ratio, Proportion, Percent, and Data Analysis

Handouts

Introduction

The GED Mathematics Test

The GED Math Test is constructed to test problem-solving and reasoning skills using real-life contexts. Marketplace, workplace, and domestic situations provide the settings for problems that require a variety of mathematical skills. To create realistic settings, the test is made up mostly of "word problems," which the examinee must interpret as mathematical problems. There are many forms of the test, and each will contain a few items that require mathematical reasoning but have no realistic context at all. There will also be items in which examinees are asked only to set up the solution, not to find the final answer. The use of calculators will be allowed on the first half of the test.

The GED Math Problem Solver and this teacher's guide present a curriculum based on the specifications of the GED Mathematics Test. Content is drawn from the strands of Number Sense and Operations, Measurement and Geometry, Data Analysis and Statistics, and Algebra and Functions. Cognitive demands of tasks represent the procedural, conceptual, and problem-solving domains. The different strands and cognitive tasks are integrated throughout the text. Thus, they provide an efficient, up-to-date course of study that prepares students for the kinds of mathematical problems that will confront them on the test. Importantly, in most cases, the test items simulate the kinds of mathematical problems students will need to solve in everyday life.

Teacher Preparation

Before you attempt to prepare students to pass the GED Math Test, you should be aware of what the test requires. The Official Practice Tests (authorized by the GED Testing Service, One Dupont Circle, N.W., Washington, D.C. 20036; http://www.gedtest.org) are the best indicators of what an actual test is like. They can be purchased through the link, Preparation Materials, at the GED website. There are numerous forms; look over as many as you can.

Notice that the test emphasizes problem solving, conceptual understanding, and reasoning more than facts and procedures. While computational skills are involved in answering many questions, they are not the focus of the assessment. In keeping with the curricula of high schools today, the test assesses the broad mathematical proficiency of the examinee, not isolated skills.

Implications for Instruction

The broad focus of the test compels us to make adjustments to the traditional basic mathematics instruction for adults. The traditional linear approach to mathematics, where students must demonstrate proficiency with one skill before they are exposed to another should be modified.

Instructional programs should do the following:

Develop number and operation sense.

Computational proficiency remains a desired skill, but does not have to loom over students as a prerequisite to higher-level thinking. For adults especially, it is more effective to acquire computational skills in the context of situations from daily life and from the perspective of mathematical reasoning. To meet the demands of the test as well as today's technological society, adult basic math students need to develop number and operation sense rather than mere procedural skill.

Promote flexibility.

Mathematical procedures are not written in stone. Algorithms vary from culture to culture; there is no one right way to do long division, for example. By building a repertoire of strategies with which to approach problems on the test, students will learn the underlying principles and see the connections that permit the flexibility that problem solving requires. Encouraging students to devise estimation and mental math strategies frees them from the tyranny of "one right way" and helps them to weave a web of understanding that values the process as well as the answer.

Build awareness of mathematical aspects of situations.

Noticing details and recognizing patterns are components of a mathematical way of thinking. They lead naturally to the algebraic symbolic skills of writing mathematical expressions and equations. Algebra, as a scheme of generalizations and connections, should be integrated throughout a GED preparation course.

Use contexts involving data and geometry.

Referring to the inter-relationships between the visual and the symbolic representations of concepts enhances learning. Apply this principle to a wide range of concepts, from characteristics of geometric figures and informational graphs of data, to representations of functions on coordinate planes.

Teach students to use calculators intelligently.

Calculating machines, embodied as computers, cash registers, or hand-held calculators, are an integral part of our daily lives as well as essential tools in the workplace. Adult basic math classrooms should promote the use of calculators to explore relationships between numbers and operations as well as to find the answer when complex computation is involved. When tedious number crunching is delegated to the calculator, students are free to focus on reasoning and strategies. In an adult math class, those without basic computational skills can participate in genuine problem-solving activities along with those with more advanced skills. Finding the answer without a calculator is not abandoned under this approach; students are encouraged to choose a method for solution (mental math, estimation, paper and pencil, or a calculator) that fits the situation.

Structure of the Student Book

There are 25 lessons arranged into four sections. Within each section, topics from arithmetic, algebra, geometry and data analysis are integrated into a cohesive whole that mixes applications with principles, and procedures with concepts. The book, as a whole, presents an efficient, yet thorough, GED preparation course that builds a solid foundation for further study in mathematics.

Lesson Design

The lessons are designed to be used in an interactive classroom setting. While it is possible for a student to work individually at his or her own pace through the lessons, this is not recommended. Make every effort to arrange for students to learn together.

Mental Math Exercises

At the beginning of most of the lessons, a small number of "warm-ups" provide an opening exercise for your students. Sometimes they will focus everyone's thoughts by reviewing concepts from the previous lesson. At other times, they will introduce the ideas being presented in the lesson.

Principles, Examples, and Problems

The examples and principles lay the groundwork for the problem sets that are interspersed throughout the lesson. Encourage students to work in pairs or groups on the problem sets after you have introduced the topic. The problems are structured so that students, with your guidance, can discover the concepts basic to the lesson. Guided discovery is the best description of what will be going on in your classroom. Tailor the lesson to the students' needs by listening carefully to the student discussions. They provide an ongoing assessment of the learning that is taking place, giving you clues to decide whether or not to insert more detailed background material or to omit topics that are already understood.

Calculator Explorations and Using Data Activities

Typically, these activities demand more thought and insight than the problems within the lessons. Guide students in making their conclusions by using questions rather than explanations. It is important *not* to explain away all the opportunities for creative reasoning and inventive strategizing.

Check Your Understanding

The problems at the end of each lesson provide an opportunity for students to check themselves as they independently solve new but related problems. This page can be homework, but will probably be more effective if done at the end of a class. If students repeat the problems just prior to the next class, they will be ready for the new topic.

GED Practice

At the end of each lesson, a page of GED-type problems shows how the topics of the lesson might appear in the actual test. Both question formats are included, multiple choice and free response, with both the standard number grid and the coordinate plane grid. In addition, calculator use is allowed on only some of the items on this page. In this way, students will become familiar with the formats and demands of the test.

Answer Key

The answers in the answer key are meant to be part of the learning process. Students are not required to use the same solution methods given in the answer key, but they can learn by comparing their methods with the ones shown.

Structure of the Teacher's Guide

This guide gives you additional materials to flesh out your instruction as well as suggestions for supplemental exercises and activities.

Objectives

The objectives give an overall view of what students will be accomplishing in the lesson.

Background

Background information for each lesson will help you and your students understand what direction the lesson takes and the reasons for a particular approach.

Lesson Recommendations and Extension Activities

The recommendations for each lesson give a starting point for discussion and ideas for different solution methods. Also included in this section of the teacher's guide are extension activities designed to help students discover and/or reinforce various principles of mathematics.

An Interactive Classroom Atmosphere

The structure of an interactive classroom can vary from teacher to teacher and class to class. It usually is some combination of teacher-directed instruction and small-group discussions. Learning goals provide the purpose, but flexibility is the key ingredient in attaining them—flexibility to find more than one way to find the answer, flexibility to build on students' invented strategies, flexibility to integrate a social science concept into a math lesson, and above all, flexibility to learn from mistakes that everyone will make.

Whenever a class is formed, you will have a number of different levels of skills and understanding. Try to make this an asset, rather than dwelling on the difficulties that it poses. In a group, students identify with each other and gain comfort in knowing they are not alone. They usually are happy to help one another, knowing that when they do, their own understanding increases. Adult students will be able to contribute unique solution strategies from their varied experiences. Most will agree that participating in a class is preferable to the lonely experience of individualized instruction, and will accept the increased responsibility for participation that it entails. Encourage your center to offer one-on-one tutoring to supplement the class experience. Students benefit from the attention to their individual needs, especially when skill proficiency is the issue.

In learning centers that must maintain an open-entry policy or those who have very few learners at a time, forming classes in the traditional sense is nearly impossible. Ingenious solutions may be necessary to achieve the interactive experience, but the results will be worth the effort.

"Seeing" Addition and Subtraction

OBJECTIVES

In this lesson, students will

- develop intuition for deciding when to add or subtract from the context of real-life problems; learn to recognize clue relationships rather than clue words
- use variables (letters in place of numbers)
- use mathematical notation to describe the mathematical elements of a situation
- use mental computation techniques based on the knowledge of basic facts and place value
- estimate sums and differences by rounding numbers first; use to check for reasonableness
- read values from a bar graph by estimating along the scale

Background

Addition and Subtraction Facts

As students progress through this lesson, you will detect areas of weakness in some students' basic addition and subtraction skills. This is normal and often simply reflects a need to practice and use those skills in various contexts. Having the facts "at one's fingertips" is very helpful when computing mentally or estimating, but merely memorizing the facts in a rote manner is usually ineffective for the long term. The following activity describes the process of noticing the patterns that are formed while constructing a table. It provides a review of the facts while it introduces an important aspect of mathematical thinking.

Handout 1:
Basic Facts

TG page 110

EXTENSION ACTIVITY

Basic Facts   (individual or in pairs)

In a tutoring session meant for those students who have substantive problems with basic addition and subtraction, help them to construct an addition table like the one on page 110 of this guide.

Ⓐ To construct the table, label the row and column headings from 0 to 9. The student then should fill in the answers that he or she knows. After doing that, make students aware of the following points:

- Adding 0 does not change the number. (Point out the first row and column.)
- Adding 1 is just like counting; find the next number. (Refer to the second row and column.)

- Adding 2 is just adding 1 twice.

- It is not necessary to fill in the answers in any particular order. In fact, by asking the student to fill in only those answers that he or she knows, you can diagnose the student's difficulties.

B As you continue to complete the table together, help the student recognize the patterns formed because of commutativity (4 + 5 is the same as 5 + 4). Talk about the odds and evens (odd + odd = even, even + even = even, odd + even = odd). Note the sums that are equal to 10 and the ones greater than 10. And note the "doubles" of each number on the diagonal of the table.

C If a student can isolate where he or she is having difficulties, show some compensatory ways to figure out the sum in case he or she forgets the answer. For example, if the student has trouble with 7 + 8 = 15, you can refer to more familiar facts: 7 + 7 and 8 + 8. The answer to 7 + 8 falls in between.

D When the table is completed correctly, allow the student to use it whenever he or she needs it.

Lesson Recommendations

PAGES 2–3

1. Picture the Situation

The beginning pages of the lesson may seem too elementary for a GED class, but their intent is to establish a fundamental notion of mathematical problem solving—understanding the problem and the relationships between the numbers in it is a critical first step.

Use pictures to help students visualize the action involved when they add or subtract. To introduce addition, emphasize the actions involved with *combine* and *join*, and use descriptive phrases like *bring together* as you discuss the problems.

Introduce subtraction through the actions of *separating* and *comparing*. The clue relationships will be the basis for deciding which operation to use in solving the problem.

You may also want to make the actions of addition and subtraction more concrete by using manipulatives, objects that can be handled by the learners so they can experience the operations in a tactile way.

PAGES 4–5

2. Write the Problem

The step of writing the problem is stressed in this book for many reasons:

- It deemphasizes the focus on finding the answer.

- It prepares students for the use of variables.

- It enables students to choose the correct response in set-up problems on the GED Test.

- It provides a stopping place to decide how to proceed to the answer. It can be critical in the self-analysis of how one learns.

Many students resist doing this step. They can get the answer without it so they view it as an unnecessary hurdle. You must persist in helping them overcome this tendency. They need to realize that the answers to individual problems, as such, are really not the important result we are working toward. Being able to write the problem is essential to being able to explain their thinking to others.

You can also use this opportunity to ease students away from the vertical to the horizontal format of writing problems. When written horizontally, the problem will be in the format in which mathematics is most often communicated, not only in writing, but also when being entered into a calculator or computer.

Variables are often used to represent an unknown or changeable quantity in everyday experiences. Ask students to look and listen for their use in commercials and news stories. They are introduced here in a gradual way so that algebra reflects the arithmetic it generalizes. Make a point of showing how the examples with variables use the same words as the examples with numbers (**Problem 6**).

PAGE 6

3. Find the Answer

As stated before, students expect that the main focus of a math class should be on this step. Encourage students to consistently focus on the prior two steps of *understanding* and *writing* the problem. Finding the answer is only one step of the process, and since students may also use calculators, it is not the step that this book emphasizes.

Sometimes the method chosen to find an answer depends on the situation and at other times on the person solving the problem. For example, the problem itself may not require a precise numerical answer (as in the case of finding the amount of paint to buy for a room). On the other hand, while a shopper in a department store would *estimate* the price of an item that is marked 25% off, he or she would not allow the cashier to estimate the price at the cash register.

Estimation and mental computation should be considered as the first options when trying to find the solution to a problem. They are the quickest and most efficient methods available, and are especially appropriate for a class of adults. Students' self-esteem will grow each week as they see what powerful tools they already have.

On page 59 of the student book, a flowchart shows the process that this book advocates for solving the problems on the GED Math Test.

PAGE 7

Adding and Subtracting Mentally

Some students will love the mental math problems from the start, but expect that most will insist that they need to write the problems in a vertical format before they know which digits they can add or subtract. Wean them away from this by pointing out the place value of the digits. More will be said about this in the next section.

The first mental math problems in this lesson (**Problem 7**) ask students to concentrate on the first digit of each number and to use basic addition and subtraction facts (2 + 3 = 5, 20 + 30 = 50, and so forth). This exercise reviews the basic facts in a way that does not insult the student. The set requiring them to focus on the end digit (**Problem 9**) may need to be explained and pictured by using one or both exercises in the following activity.

Handout 2:
Hundreds Chart

TG page 111

EXTENSION ACTIVITY

Hundreds Chart (whole class)

Make a transparency of the hundreds chart (TG page 111) to project on an overhead, or give each student a copy to follow. The purpose of this activity is to show (through patterns that occur in the array of numbers) what is involved when you "carry" in addition and "borrow" in subtraction. (Carrying and borrowing are sometimes called **regrouping**.) The first column of problems (**Problem 9Ⓐ**) starts with 6 + 8 = 14.

PROBLEM 9Ⓐ

1. Circle the 6.
2. Count 8 places, landing on the 14.
3. Put a box around 14.

Repeat the process with 36 + 8 and again with 56 + 8. Ask students to notice the pattern: The numbers being boxed are in the next row from the circled numbers (a jump to the next tens digit), and they all end in 4 (which is 2 less than 6). By the time students get to 126 + 8, they won't need the chart.

1	2	3	4	5	⑥	7	8	9	10
11	12	13	[14]	15	16	17	18	19	20
21	22	23	24	25	26	27	28	29	30
31	32	33	34	35	㊱	37	38	39	40
41	42	43	[44]	45	46	47	48	49	50
51	52	53	54	55	㊶	57	58	59	60
61	62	63	[64]	65	66	67	68	69	70
71	72	73	74	75	76	77	78	79	80
81	82	83	84	85	㊆	87	88	89	90
91	92	93	[94]	95	96	97	98	99	100

Students may already know the pattern that occurs when 9 is added to a number. If so, ask a student to illustrate it on the chart for **Problem 9Ⓒ**.

PROBLEM 9Ⓑ

Similarly, borrowing is demonstrated by this visual aid for 11 − 7 = 4.

1. Circle 11.
2. Count 7 places back to subtract.
3. Put a box around 4.

Repeat for 31 − 7. Ask students to describe the pattern being shown.

You may encounter students who have developed a mental block about the carrying and borrowing processes. Alternative ways to compute are shown

1	2	3	[4]	5	6	7	8	9	10
⑪	12	13	14	15	16	17	18	19	20
21	22	23	[24]	25	26	27	28	29	30
㉛	32	33	34	35	36	37	38	39	40
41	42	43	44	45	46	47	48	49	50
51	52	53	54	55	56	57	58	59	60
61	62	63	64	65	66	67	68	69	70
71	72	73	74	75	76	77	78	79	80
81	82	83	84	85	86	87	88	89	90
91	92	93	94	95	96	97	98	99	100

in the Appendix of the student book (page 298). Stress that these methods are just as good as the traditional algorithms. This book often shows more than one way to solve a problem so that the student can choose the way that fits the problem and the situation. Encourage students to be insightful and flexible rather than to be at the mercy of a single method.

4. Check for Reasonableness

In this step, students learn specific techniques for making estimates that can serve as a basis for judging whether or not an answer is reasonable.

Calculator Exploration

Use this first calculator exploration to demonstrate that the calculator will be used for instruction as well as for finding the answers. The aim of this exploration is to have a little fun while learning to recognize the different place values.

The estimating that is covered in this lesson is called, appropriately, **front-end estimation**. The traditional guidelines for rounding are summarized but students are also asked to physically mark the position of a number on the number line and see what number it is "closest to." The role that the halfway marks play corresponds to the role of the 5 in the guidelines. Encourage the kind of common sense thinking that will tell students how to round in these cases.

Problem 10 includes numbers that involve the transition between 900 and 1,000. It would be helpful to use the expressions "ten hundred" and "eleven hundred" for these positions on the number line of hundreds. When discussing how the place-value system works, show how these expressions equal one thousand and one thousand, one hundred, respectively.

The same concept arises again with the number line of 10s in **Problem 11**.

Using Data

The reasoning that was used in placing numbers on the number line is applied here when reading (estimating) values from a graph. Stress the technique of establishing halfway marks between the tic marks that are shown on the graph.

Show students how to use the corner (a right angle) of a piece of paper to ensure that they remain strictly horizontal when looking back to the scale. Line up one edge along the vertical axis and the perpendicular edge so that it touches the point in question.

GED Practice

The Heat Index Table is a reduced version of the one on page 291 of the Appendix. The tasks in **Problems 3–5** require locating the relevant numbers in the table, a basic data reading skill. Use the large table for additional practice, if needed.

The directions for using the number grid on page 282 will also appear with every form of the GED Test. The directions explain how answers can be entered into the grid in different ways and still be considered correct. For example, 102, the answer to **Problem 3**, can start with the 1 in the left-most column, the next column, or the middle column. It is not necessary to put a decimal point at the end of a whole number.

Grouping to Add More Than Two Numbers

OBJECTIVES

This lesson will help students to

- use the associative law and parentheses to group addends
- write and evaluate algebraic expressions
- estimate sums involving money using compatible pairs and grouping
- use calculators to find precise sums
- recognize the relative size of decimal numerals
- interpolate to determine the length of a bar in a bar graph between two given values

Background

Flexibility in Adding Numbers

Flexibility is important to problem solving. Students must be able to use a variety of methods to find the answer to a problem, especially when estimating. To be flexible, however, your students must develop confidence with respect to the fundamental principles of mathematics. For example, if students are certain that they can change the order and grouping of numbers when they add, they will see that there are many ways to approach problems. For this reason, the **commutative** and **associative** properties of addition are explained and then used to find both precise and approximate answers.

Number Sense

Numeracy involves being comfortable with numbers. This lesson explicitly points out the idea of compatible pairs of numbers for addition, benchmarks that offer some easy numbers that are comfortable to work with when adding and subtracting. (Numbers that add to 10 are compatible, as are numbers that add to 100.) Compatible pairs are useful when looking for steps that can be done mentally, especially when dealing with money.

Lesson Recommendations

PAGE 13

Mental Math

Most of the lessons that follow will be preceded by a set of mental math exercises that are a warm-up to the lesson topic or a quick review of an earlier lesson. If your students respond well to these, you may wish to construct your own groups of problems to supplement those given. For example, you could extend this set to include pairs of numbers that add to 100. Try to group the problems so that they have a common theme or lead to a concept.

PAGES 13-14

Perimeters

Perimeter, a topic from geometry and measurement, offers a concrete application for adding more than two numbers. With perimeters, you can teach students to use the associative law by grouping the addends into compatible pairs. (Students are not required to know the names of the laws, only when to apply them.)

Try to convince your students to take time to analyze a problem first, instead of immediately beginning to add from left to right. When a calculator is not being used, time spent thinking about how to regroup the numbers to make adding easier offers a huge advantage. "Look before you leap" is a recurring theme in this book.

PAGE 14

Grouping with Variables

This section reintroduces the concept of variables from **Lesson 1**. The two perimeter examples show how to write the expression, group the numbers, add them, and indicate the remaining addition to be done.

EXTENSION ACTIVITY

Understanding x   (whole class or small group)

Ⓐ Put varying numbers of strips of colored paper into same-sized envelopes. Seal each envelope, and write an x on it.

Ⓑ *Writing an expression.* Give each student (or group) one envelope and four additional individual strips of paper. Ask how many strips of paper each one has. Without opening the envelopes, they can say only that they have x + 4 strips of paper. Write this expression on the board as a heading for a table.

x	x + 4

Ⓒ *Evaluating an expression.* Ask each student or group to open the envelope and determine the value (each different) of x. Again, ask how many strips of paper each has.

Ⓓ Let a representative from each group fill in one row of the table, while explaining, for example, that *if* x is 7, x + 4 is 11.

PAGE 15

Evaluating Expressions

If you have done the extension activity, the exercises will serve as applications of the ideas and will provide valuable practice. The word *substitute* is important. To promote the idea of a variable as an unknown placeholder, you may also want to use "whatever" or "who knows what?" in place of *x*.

Using Data

Here the students are asked to notice the pattern in the rows of numbers that represent shoe sizes in different countries. They notice the pattern, write an expression that defines the relationship for every number in the table, and finally evaluate the expression for a value *not* on the table.

I've included the row of European sizes to serve as a comparison. Say that students volunteer that $x + 30$, for example, is the expression that represents the pattern. Ask them to show that this expression works for all values in the table. Since it does not, it cannot be correct.

PAGES 16–17

Estimating and Calculating with Money

This section focuses on learning math for the way we use it. Many situations in our lives do not require an exact total. If the precise answer is needed, either a cash register or a calculator can provide it. What is important for most of us is to be able to find an approximate total to provide a quick check against carelessness.

The only real rule of estimating is that you must simplify the problem enough to be able to do it in your head. Of course, an estimate that is accurate enough for the situation is the goal. The students are sharpening their mental skills so that they can feel comfortable with estimating and mental calculating.

In **front-end estimation**, focus on the digit that tells the most about the size of a number—the left-most digit. Sometimes an estimate needs to be refined by first **rounding** or **grouping** the cents into dollars. Rounding is more appropriate when the values are near the extremes ($1.99 or $4.07) (**Problem 8**), and grouping works better with intermediate values (when the cents add up to approximately a dollar, as in **Problem 9**).

These different methods of estimating offer students a choice so they can be flexible in their thinking and can choose the one that will give a more accurate answer. However, no one estimate is the only right estimate. Many students will have developed strategies of their own to apply to these situations, and some of their strategies may be more practical than those presented here. Be sure to maintain a classroom atmosphere where all reasonable estimates are acceptable, and encourage explanations of unique methods.

PAGES 18–19

Money and Decimals

Students often have trouble understanding the concept of a decimal, but they know about money. Use this knowledge to help students make the connection between money and pure decimals, and to make important observations about the relative size of decimals and how to add and subtract them.

Calculator Exploration

The calculator exploration asks students to first use their experience with money to tell the total value of the coins. Then it asks them to enter the values into the calculator, coin by coin, and see whether the calculator agrees with their sum. The point of the exploration is to reinforce the connection between the value of coins and decimals. While it may be tempting to explain the concept in advance, allow the mistakes to happen. Expect that some students will forget the decimal point and others will ponder whether or not the zero is necessary. At the end of the exercise, ask students to make a generalization about the zeroes. (The zero before a decimal point is usually included in written text only to give a signal that a decimal point is present. Adding (or omitting) *trailing* zeroes in decimal fractions does not change the value.) If students still seem uncomfortable with the ideas, do the following activity.

EXTENSION ACTIVITY

Understanding Zeros in Decimals　　　　　(individual or in pairs)

Guide students to discover whether or not the zeros in a decimal are critical to its value by using the following activity with their calculators.

Ⓐ	6.40	64.00	6.04
Ⓑ	1.50	1.05	
Ⓒ	46.20	46.02	
Ⓓ	12.00	1.20	1.02

1. Students should enter each number separately into their calculators, followed by the equals sign. (Remind students to clear their calculators before each entry.)

2. Notice the number that is displayed on their calculators after the equals sign is entered. Is the 0 retained? If yes, the 0 is critical. If not, it is not critical.

PAGE 20

Using Data

This activity asks students to determine the length of bars to represent numbers that do not correspond to the grid marks of the graph. It is an estimation task equivalent to placing numbers on a number line, but also one that calls attention to the structure of a bar graph. The length of the bar is the characteristic of the graph that makes the connection between the vertical scale and the listing of states on the bottom. In a later activity, students will be asked to determine the values that should be listed on the vertical scale.

PAGES 20–22

Comparing Decimal Numbers

Review the meaning of the inequality signs and use **Problem 12** to make sure that everyone understands the directionality of $<$ and $>$.

The connection between the relative size of numbers and setting up the order in a subtraction expression is explored in **Problem 14** and in the **Calculator Exploration**. Even though negatives have not yet been discussed in this book, students should be able to recognize how the calculator is telling them which number is greater.

Handout 7:
*Tenths/Hundredths
Grids*

TG page 116

EXTENSION ACTIVITY

Understanding Decimal Places
(whole class)

Visual explanations often carry more meaning than verbal ones, especially if you have students with limited fluency in English. Use the tenths and hundredths grids found on page 116 of this book to illustrate the previous principle—adding trailing zeros does not change the value of a decimal. It is a technique that is used to give decimal numbers an equal number of digits so that comparing them is easier.

1. Make a transparency of the page and cut it so that you have separate transparencies of the tenths grid and the hundredths grid.

2. On an overhead projector, superimpose one grid over the other to show that the entire square of each grid equals one.

3. One possible presentation might be the following:

Shade 3 tenths on the tenths grid and superimpose the hundredths grid showing that it is equal to 30 hundredths. Write $0.3 = 0.30$ on the board to make sure that everyone understands the significance of what was shown.

Next, shade 25 hundredths on the hundredths grid. Superimpose it on the tenths grid that you used before and ask the students to summarize what you are showing. $(0.3 > 0.25)$

4. Be ready to use the grids to explain answers in **Problem 13**.

TENTHS GRID

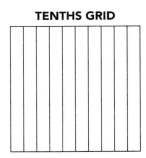

HUNDREDTHS GRID

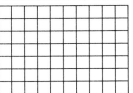

Calculating and Estimating with a Checking Account

(small groups or in pairs)

Some people use calculators to balance their checkbook with their bank statement. Other people may use estimation to keep track of the activity in their account. The following activity lets students see how effective each method is and helps them decide which method would be more appropriate for them.

MONTHLY STATEMENT

Date	Debits	Credits	Transaction Description	Balance
9/04		1500.00	opening deposit	1500.00
9/04	5.00		check printing fee	_____
9/08	178.32		check #101	_____
9/10	50.00		cash withdrawal	_____
9/13	36.21		check #102	_____
9/16	23.00		check #103	_____
9/18	50.00		cash withdrawal	_____
9/26		148.33	deposit	_____
9/27	50.00		cash withdrawal	_____
9/30		4.48	interest payment	_____
9/30	3.56		monthly maintenance charge	_____

1. Have students use the monthly statement above to estimate the balance in the account at the end of the month. They could do this mentally by doing these steps:

   - Working with the debits column, group amounts that add to approximately $100, and then add these groups together.
   - Estimate the total in the credits column. Finally, find the difference between these totals.

2. Have students use their calculators to find the exact balance that should appear on the last line in the balance column by finding the interim balances one transaction at a time.

3. Now have students compare their estimates from step 1 with the final figure they arrived at for the monthly statement ($1,256.72). Discuss the difference between the amounts and possible causes for the differences. Discuss whether or not students would be comfortable estimating when they check their own statements. What is the reason for checking—to catch a computation error or to find some other gross error like putting an amount in the wrong column?

Equivalent Equations: Addition and Subtraction

OBJECTIVES

To apply and strengthen their understanding of the relationship between addition and subtraction, students will

- write equivalent equations
- translate problem situations into mathematical equations
- solve equations using "fact families" or algebraic techniques

Background

Using Equations

This lesson introduces the use of equations to solve problems. Equations contain an equals sign and can be *solved* for the value of the unknown, whereas expressions, with no equals sign, can only be *evaluated*. By using variables in equations that represent the situations in word problems mathematically, students learn a method that will allow them to solve more complicated problems. They will be able to solve problems even if they don't see a path to the solution from the outset. The key is to capture the mathematical essence of the situation in symbols.

When working with variables, the step of finding the answer becomes one of solving the equation, that is, finding the number that makes it true. At its simplest level, solving equations can be used as a review of addition facts. By asking a student to solve the equation $3 + x = 10$, you are asking, "What number, added to 3, equals 10?" The student who does not want to admit needing to review the basic facts may enjoy this approach because he or she is "doing algebra."

Rearranging equations so that the variable is alone on its side of the equation is a strategy based on the idea of arithmetic "fact families." Using this strategy develops a greater sense of the relationship between the operations of addition and subtraction, an important goal in itself. It requires the use of common sense.

The more formal algebraic properties of equality are also introduced here as an alternate method of solving equations. "More than one way" could be a subtitle describing this book. By comparing the interim steps and the results of using the algebraic rule to those of rearranging the equation using fact families, students see the basis for the rule and gain confidence that mathematics does indeed make sense.

Lesson Recommendations

PAGE 25

Mental Math

This group of mental math exercises reviews translating literal expressions into mathematical operations. The exercises prepare the student for writing equations later in this lesson.

PAGES 26–27

Writing Equivalent Equations Using "Fact Families"

You can make the concept of equivalent equations less threatening to students by referring them to elementary applications that they will all recognize. First, remind students that when they learned the addition facts, they also learned the subtraction facts. Illustrate with a simple example:

By learning $2 + 3 = 5$, they knew $5 - 2 = 3$ and $5 - 3 = 2$.

Second, they used this relationship when they checked subtraction answers by using addition.

RECALL		IN EQUATION FORM:
	$\begin{array}{r} 100 \\ -74 \\ \hline 26 \\ +74 \\ \hline 100 \end{array}$	$100 - 74 = 26$
		CHECK:
		$26 + 74 = 100$

The symbol of the triangle provides a visual representation of the connection between the three numbers in an addition fact, the addends on one level and the sum by itself on another. It gives the students a physical place to put the numbers in the relation. In my own teaching experience, I have seen the effectiveness of this approach in removing the barriers to understanding for many students. They use the symbol until they are comfortable with the abstraction of the equations.

PAGES 27–29

Writing Equations to Solve Problems

The words *solving word problems* have struck terror into many algebra students, perhaps even into some math teachers. However, unlike the coin and age problems of traditional algebra, the word problems in this book describe practical, everyday situations where math is required to find an answer. With the right approach, a synergy between the applications and the procedures can develop, where the combination of the two will be more powerful than the sum of its parts. The applications from daily life provide motivation and meaning for adults with similar experiences. The steps of the procedure—understand the problem, write the equation, find the answer, and check for reasonableness, the same as that introduced in the first lesson—become a comfortable approach. The situations become more complex later in the book; use the simpler ones in this lesson to establish the mechanics of a thought process that will also be effective later.

The most difficult step for students usually is writing the equation. Here are some points that may be helpful.

1. Assign a variable. Have students focus first on what the question is asking for, and then assign a letter (variable) to the unknown quantity. Without this step, the whole process loses its logic.

2. Reread the problem, looking for a sentence that describes the relationship between the known quantities and the unknown.

3. Place the equals sign. Each side of an equation has the same value. Look for places where you can substitute the verb *is* or *are*; these are likely places for the equals sign.

4. Translate the words into mathematical symbols. Compare this to translating between languages. Sometimes you can translate literally; other times you must rearrange the words. Often, rearranging into chronological order makes the process of translating easier.

Throughout this book we will explore many problem-solving strategies. However, there is no strategy that eliminates the need to *understand the problem*. If you suspect that your students are having difficulties because they don't understand what they are reading, take some additional time to discuss the problem in other words. Talk about the situation from different perspectives and in students' own words (substituting the variable for the unknown quantity during your discussions) before you begin trying to interpret it as a mathematics problem.

The two techniques in this lesson—following the action of the problem and using a known relationship as a guideline—will help the student who does not have the insight and experience to be able to analyze a situation. Both techniques provide a structure or framework for writing the original equation.

PAGES 30–31

Solving Equations

The sight of equations with variables is intimidating to many students. We try to calm their fears by providing a transition between the arithmetic that they are comfortable with and the algebraic formalities.

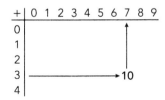

Equations of the form $3 + x = 10$ represent the "missing addend" interpretation of subtraction. You can demonstrate an elementary version of this by using the addition table found on page 110 of this guide. For example, to explain the problem $3 + x = 10$, locate the 3 in the row headings and move sideways into the table entries until you come to the 10. Then follow that column back up to its heading to find the value for x (7).

We begin by teaching students to use the fact families and common sense to manipulate equations, before we introduce the transformation rules of algebra. In this way, the student develops an intuitive understanding before being asked to follow what may seem to be purely mechanical procedures.

PAGE 32

Rewriting Equations Using Algebraic Rules

The generalizations or properties of algebra present a logical framework that is the basis for much of the mathematics to follow. Attempt to give reasons for the rules as they are presented. Here there are two ideas to emphasize:

1. What you do to one side of an equation, you must also do to the other side so that they remain equal.

2. The operation that you do to both sides is determined by the original equation. You "do" whatever it takes to "undo" the operation that is shown because you want the variable to be alone.

Some students find it easier to write the numbers that they are adding or subtracting directly beneath the original equation. That is acceptable.

Geometry Topics

OBJECTIVES

Students will

- apply algebraic problem-solving techniques to geometry topics
- recognize and measure right, acute, obtuse, and straight angles
- use the facts about complementary and supplementary angles to find a missing angle measure
- use the fact that the angles of a triangle sum to 180° to find the missing measure of one angle
- recognize the equality of vertical and corresponding angles
- apply knowledge of angle equality and reasoning skills to complex figures

Background

Reasoning with Geometry and Algebra

This lesson introduces some definitions, vocabulary, and relationships involving angles. Moreover, it asks students to apply the algebraic techniques of equation solving to geometric questions and challenges them to reason and draw conclusions from examples and theorems. This integrated approach, where one field informs the other, nurtures a holistic understanding of topics that eases the transfer of skills from one setting to another.

Lesson Recommendations

PAGES 38–39

Mental Math

These problems, which are set up as equations, give students a chance to invent some unique ways to find answers mentally. Ask them to explain their thinking.

Angles

The measure of an angle is the "amount of turning" that takes place between its two sides. Demonstrate this on the board or overhead projector by placing the point of a pencil on the vertex of an angle while the pencil lies along one side of the angle. Then rotate it, with the point fixed on the vertex, to the other side.

The facts about the measure of angles can be made real to some students by reminding them of the everyday uses this concept has in our language. "He did a 180" describes a person who changed his mind to the other point of view. "She came full circle" describes a person who came back to her original view.

Using protractors to measure angles can be very instructive (as a hands-on activity) while discussing right, straight, obtuse, and acute angles. Verify, for example, that the measure of the acute angle falls between 0° and 90°.

EXTENSION ACTIVITY

Estimating Angles
(whole class)

To develop estimation skills with angles, have students construct an estimating protractor. You may want to draw a sketch of each step on the board or have students follow along as you do the activity yourself.

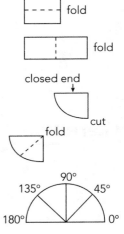

1. Fold a piece of paper precisely in half, taking care to line up the edges.

2. Fold the paper again, aligning the edges with the previous fold.

3. Start cutting on the closed end of the paper, and cut a curved line to opposite bottom edge.

4. Fold the paper in half once more, forming a "pie wedge."

5. Unfold the paper twice, so half a circle is showing, and label the fold lines with the corresponding degrees.

Ask students, "How would you label the protractor so you could measure in both directions as with a standard protractor?"

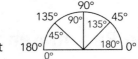

6. Add the second set of numbers to the protractor.

Discuss how students would know which set of numbers to use. Only one of the measures *makes sense* for the angle being measured. The angles in **Problem 1** can be measured using these "estimating protractors."

Students should also be able to judge an angle's approximate size (within 30°) just by looking at it.

PAGES 40–41

Complementary and Supplementary Angles

Students should try to learn the meanings of the words **complementary** and **supplementary angles** in this lesson, not to be able to write a definition, but to be able to use them in context.

The exercises that use equations to find the answers to geometric questions give you a chance to emphasize that finding answers is not the only reason we are studying mathematics. Here the geometric context gives a perfect situation to review and advance the students' comfort with algebraic symbol manipulation. **Problem 6**, on the other hand, challenges students' problem-solving skills; it is more like a puzzle than a serious problem. Mathematics involves many problems without realistic contexts that are meant to develop reasoning power.

PAGES 42–43

Triangles

The fact that the sum of the angles of a triangle equals 180° generates the obvious problems that are here and are often included in many standardized tests. You can help students to accept it as being true with the activity that follows. You can find other similar activities in NCTM (National Council of Teachers of Mathematics) publications.

> ### EXTENSION ACTIVITY
>
> **Adding Angles** (small groups or in pairs)
>
> Do this extension activity only after students are sure that a straight angle measures 180°. This activity uses that principle.
>
> 1. Cut out a variety of different-shaped triangles, then give each student a triangle.
>
>
>
> 2. Have students mark or color each vertex (corner) of their triangle.
>
> 3. Instruct students to tear each triangle into three pieces, each containing a vertex.
>
> 4. Have students line the pieces up so that the original vertex angles about each other on a straight line, perhaps the edge of the desk. In every case, the sum of the three angles will make a straight line.
>
>

The formula, $\angle a + \angle b + \angle c = 180°$, can be rearranged to find the missing value. Of course, students resist the formal approach and want to merely find the answer in a two-step procedure. However, it is important to pay attention to the formal algebraic representation of the problem because it exemplifies an important principle.

Calculator Exploration

This exploration leads to the discovery that the minus sign preceding the parentheses "distributes" to both addends. That is, subtracting the sum of the two numbers is equivalent to subtracting both of them separately. Violating this principle is one of the common errors that students make so, of course, you can expect problems involving parentheses after a minus sign to appear in tests.

Reasoning Activity

Although this reasoning activity does not constitute a formal proof of the theorem about external angles (because it uses specific numbers instead of variables), it does demand similar reasoning skills.

PAGES 44–45

Special Types of Angles

When parallel lines are crossed by a transversal, eight angles are formed. The positions determine whether the angles are either equal or supplementary. Note, however, that this is dependent on the lines being parallel. Students should not *assume* lines are parallel or perpendicular just because they look that way. The fact must be stated explicitly or be deducible from the given information.

The Number Line and the Coordinate Grid

OBJECTIVES

Students will

- recognize the order relationship with negative numbers
- add and subtract on the number line, using negative as well as positive numbers
- name the position of points on the coordinate grid, using Cartesian coordinates

Background

Working with Integers

In this lesson, the operations of addition and subtraction are extended to all the integers, positive and negative and zero. Because your students need concrete representations of the concept of negative numbers, relevant applications are stressed. At the same time, the algebraic methods of adding and subtracting are generalized for the student.

Graphing on the 2-dimensional coordinate plane is introduced as a natural extension of the number line. The positioning of points in all four quadrants is stressed here, and ordered pairs (x, y) are used as a way to locate points on a plane.

I advise you to use the GED answer grid only for recording answers and not for instruction about the coordinate plane. The circles in the answer grid give the impression that the points where x and y are integers are the only points that exist on the coordinate plane. In fact, the coordinate plane consists of all real values of x and y—which includes the fractional and decimal values between integers.

Lesson Recommendations

PAGE 48

Mental Math

Use the mental math exercises to show students that by estimating, they know more than an approximate answer. Point out to students that if they use $20 + 13$ as an estimate for $18 + 13$ in **Problem 1**, for example, they also know that the exact answer *is less than* their estimate.

The Number Line

Use the diagram to introduce the number line and the presence of negative numbers. Discuss the symmetry centered at zero. Remind students that anything to the left of a value on the number line is less than that value. Discuss the meaning of the arrows at both ends of the number line.

PAGES 49–50

Handout 3:
Number Lines

TG page 112

Adding and Subtracting on the Number Line

The number line is an important visual aid for this topic. It serves as a concrete representation of the real numbers and their order. The students will become familiar with it here and will be able to build on their understanding when fractions are studied in **Section 3**. Handout 3 (TG page 112) has drawings of number lines to make it easier for you to use them throughout the book. Make copies for your students so they can label them with numbers that are convenient for the problem they are considering.

EXTENSION ACTIVITY

Visualizing Checking Account Activity   (small groups or in pairs)

Revisit the checking account activity (Calculating and Estimating with a Checking Account) on page 12 of this guide. Label a number line from 0 to 1,600 and indicate each transaction as a movement on the line. Depositing money is the addition of a positive, and writing a check can be interpreted as either subtracting a positive or adding a negative.

The physical movements back and forth as well as estimating the size of the movements will help students to internalize the ideas from this lesson, often treated only as abstract concepts.

PAGE 51

Calculator Exploration

Before expecting students to notice the pattern while subtracting a negative, make sure that they understand how to use the **+/−** key. The generalization that subtracting a negative has the same result as adding a positive is often difficult to accept without a physical example. Some will be discussed in the next section. For now, let the calculator do some convincing.

Students will get more practice using their calculators with negatives in **Problem 6**.

Using the Number Line

Use **Problem 5❸** as a physical example of the validity of the generalization made above. Emphasize that the problem asks for the *difference* between the recorded and the windchill temperatures, so it is a subtraction problem. As a mathematical expression, it would be written as $12 - (-10)$. Comparing the mathematical expression to what is obvious from looking at the thermometer, it is clear that subtracting a negative gets the same result as adding a positive. For additional practice, ask what the difference would be on Thursday and Friday if the recorded temperature were 3 degrees.

Wind Chill Chart
(small groups or in pairs)

A complete Wind Chill Chart is located on page 291 of the Appendix. At the least, it is a wonderful source for more questions like those in **Problem 5**. You may want to make problems more meaningful by using your local winter temperatures and wind speeds from the newspaper. To encourage students to analyze patterns in tables of numbers like these, you could ask them questions like the following:

Follow the row of wind-chill temperatures to the right of a 35-mph wind. Subtract each entry from the one just before it in that row. Describe your results. Do the same thing with the row of temperatures that are to the right of 5 mph. Can you find a row where the difference between the successive entries is always the same number?

Now look at the columns of temperatures. In which column do you see the greatest difference between the entry at the top of the chart and the one at the bottom? Describe how the difference between each successive entry changes as you move from top to bottom of the chart.

You can find more information on wind chill at www.erh.noaa.gov.

PAGES 52–55

The Coordinate Grid

To introduce the concept of locating points by means of coordinates, you could use a map and locate points of interest by using the locator. (For example, one map shows Austin, Texas, at E-27 on the map of Texas. These coordinates will vary depending on which map you use). This analogy is not strictly parallel to a coordinate grid, because on a map, the spaces are labeled, and on a Cartesian plane, the lines are labeled. But, this method will still help prepare students to find a point by projecting perpendicularly from the axis values.

Introduce the Cartesian plane by studying the diagram. Note the symmetry about zero. Discuss the four quadrants that result from the intersection of the axes. Stressing that the starting point is always the origin (0, 0), begin locating points in the first quadrant. Ask students: "Where are the negatives? How would you get to a point in the second quadrant?" The region to the left of the origin is negative just as it was on the number line. Characterize the points in each of the quadrants as indicated by the sketch below.

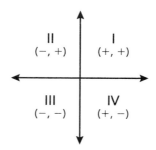

After students have completed **Problems 7** and **8**, discuss the points that lie *on* the axes. Ask students: "What characteristic do points that lie on the *x*-axis have in common?" "What is the same about every ordered pair that describes points on the *y*-axis?"

Problems 9 and **10** offer glimpses into some coordinate plane topics that go beyond simply locating points. There is no dedicated instruction on these topics because adults who can use their common sense can likely answer the questions.

PAGE 57

GED Practice

The directions for using the coordinate plane grid to record answers are found on page 283 in the Appendix. The directions will also be included in every form of the GED Test. Notice that it is only possible to record points whose *x*- and *y*-value are integers (natural numbers, their opposites, and zero).

Test-Taking Tips

OBJECTIVES

Students will

- review the methods covered in this unit
- evaluate their progress using the type of problems that will be on the GED Test

Lesson Recommendations

PAGE 58

Mental Math

The mental math exercises represent many of the strategies that were presented in this section. A non-homogeneous grouping like this is a good assessment of whether or not real learning took place.

PAGES 58–61

Two Problem-Solving Tips

The problem-solving steps are reviewed and then summarized in a flow chart. You may want to enlarge this chart and post it in your classroom.

Two general tips that can prepare students for the test-taking experience are illustrated with some sample problems.

1. Estimate first. It is a valuable time saver as well as a check for reasonableness.

2. Be prepared for the possibility that some items will not offer enough information to find an answer.

PAGES 62–63

Check Your Skills

The problems in this set are structured like the problems on the actual GED Test, but they test the student only on the addition and subtraction concepts presented in this section. Students have seen both the standard number grid and the coordinate plane grid previously so they should be comfortable recording answers on them.

The demands of this set of items include tasks that should be familiar, but problem settings that may not be. This is to stimulate students to apply what they have learned to a new, but similar, situation—the test of real learning in terms of problem solving. To simulate actual test conditions, the students should have no more than 15 minutes to complete these problems.

After the problems have been checked, there should be a full discussion of every problem. The individual students' methods of solution should be explored. You should look for and point out the valid aspects of their reasoning, even if errors were made, so students will still be encouraged.

Notice that calculators were allowed for **Problem 3** where computation is not even necessary to find the answer. Calculator-neutral items will be included in the calculator half of the GED Test; students should not expect to use the calculator on every item.

Some computation skills were required to answer **Problems 5**, **7**, and **8** even though calculators were not allowed. This will also be true in the GED Math Test. In some cases, estimation can help to find the answer. In others, fundamental computation skills are necessary. The GED Testing Service recognizes that a high school graduate should be able to demonstrate those skills.

Problem 9 uses some of the information from the Electoral College Votes table on page 295 in the Appendix that shows the number of electoral votes for each state in every election that was based on the 1990 census. Discuss this social science topic by going to the Archives Website to see what changes were made to these numbers as a result of the 2000 census.

Self Reflection

After checking their answers and discussing the problems, encourage students to take note of where they individually have made progress and where they still need work. Students may want to make lists of their individual perceived weaknesses in math that they expect to overcome. As the course proceeds, invite students to chart their progress in a way that is meaningful to them.

"Seeing" Multiplication and Division

OBJECTIVES

Students will

- develop intuition for deciding from the context of real-life problems when to multiply or divide
- recognize and write multiplication and division problems in a variety of formats
- use variables in setting up problems
- translate verbal problems into mathematical notation
- recognize patterns present in multiples and formulate divisibility rules
- use knowledge of basic facts to develop techniques for mental computation and estimation

Background

Multiplication and Division Facts

Quick recall of the multiplication facts of numbers 1 through 10 is important for success with math. Students will also benefit from knowing the facts for 11 and 12.

Work individually with students who are struggling with the basic combinations. As you did with addition, help the student construct a personal multiplication table like the one on page 110 of this guide (see TG pages 2−3 for instructions). Use mathematical reasons (see below) to give hints and ask questions that prompt them to complete the array. The student can then use the table when needed.

1. Instruct the student to fill in the answers he or she already knows. Remind them that multiplying by 2 is the same as doubling the number.

2. As you proceed, point out the patterns that occur.

   a) For example, note the symmetry about the diagonal of perfect squares. This is because multiplication is commutative. (If you fold the paper on that diagonal, the numbers that fall on each other will be equal.)

   b) You could also build on the example of adding 8s from the first lesson. Find each successive multiple of 8 by adding 8 to the previous one ($8 \times 3 = 24$: $24 + 8 = 32$, so 8×4 must be 32).

Many people have the most difficulty with the 16 answers in the bottom right square of the multiplication table. This group can be made less intimidating by the following tips:

1. Diagonally divide the square containing these 16 products into two symmetric halves. The numbers on the diagonal (perfect squares) are critical ones to know without hesitation.

2. The shaded products are the same as the upper half, so there are really only 10 facts to learn, instead of 16.

3. The starred (*) numbers are multiples of 9. Point out that the digits of each multiple of 9 add up to 9 or a multiple of 9.

4. That leaves only three more facts to memorize—the worst for most people being $7 \times 8 = 56$. Use this fact as often as you can in your realistic classroom examples. The student book also uses this tactic of constantly barraging the student with the facts that are troublesome.

Lesson Recommendations

PAGES 64–65

Mental Math

The purpose of these mental math exercises is to lay the groundwork that will connect repeated addition to multiplication.

1. Picture the Situation

As with addition and subtraction, the emphasis here is on the relationships of *combining equal* groups for multiplication and *separating* into *equal* groups for division.

As a second interpretation, demonstrate multiplication as repeated addition and division as repeated subtraction. **Example C** on page 65 pictures this, as it shows division as an operation that determines the number of equal-sized groups in a quantity. (How many times can you subtract 8?) **Example D**, in contrast, uses division to determine the size of a given number of groups. It does not lend itself to the interpretation of division as repeated subtraction.

PAGES 66–67

2. Write the Problem

Whenever you read a division problem aloud, stress the preposition *by*, as in "45 divided *by* 9." It is also helpful to restate the division problem by asking, "How many 9s are there in 45?" Being familiar with this interpretation will help the answers make sense when dividing by numbers less than 1 in the next section.

In **Problem 4☉**, your students may note that the answers given on the calculator differ only slightly: one answer has a negative sign in front, while the other answer doesn't. They have seen this before in an earlier calculator exploration, an example of the following fact: $(a - b) = -(b - a)$. However, you may need to remind students that 22 does not equal -22.

Notation

Students may not be familiar with using the form $\frac{45}{9}$ to indicate "45 divided *by* 9." Some are likely to respond (with some anxiety), "But these are fractions!" You should agree, but explain that the fraction bar is also a way to represent division.

Explain the advantages of the vertical notation by comparing the placement of the numbers in $\frac{45}{9}$ and $9\overline{)45}$. It is easier to read the division problem in the correct order when the vertical notation is used (top to bottom), "45 divided by 9." Students already learned from **Problem 4** that it is important for the order to be correct when using the calculator.

The division "house" notation is not used except for long division problems. Your students need to become familiar with the vertical notation as they divide mentally and estimate. The pedagogical advantages of using the vertical notation will become apparent as your students move seamlessly into the study of fractions in later chapters.

PAGE 68

Translating Words to Problems

Note that addition and subtraction problems also are included in the examples of mathematical expressions. You should point out the similarities (for example, addition and multiplication are both combining operations), as well as the differences (for example, multiplication requires equal groups) across the operations.

Problem 7 is a challenging one. Be prepared with actual objects to manipulate or some ideas for sketches that will help students decide whether the words ask them to combine or separate.

EXTENSION ACTIVITY

Everyday Multiplication and Division (whole class)

After you have isolated some of the multiplication and division facts that are troublesome to your students, choose one fact, say, $6 \times 8 = 48$. As a homework assignment, ask students to find a situation in their own lives that can be represented by this problem. One student may notice that there are 48 sodas in 8 six-packs; another may earn $6 per hour and work 8 hours a day, earning $48 per day. This activity reverses the book's procedure of asking students to write the problem that describes the situation.

Extend the activity into a discussion of how division and multiplication are inverse operations (the topic of **Lesson 9**). For example, use the student examples to ask a related question, "If you need 48 cans of soda, how many 6-packs should you buy?" Show that the student examples have value, perhaps greater than the ones in the text.

PAGE 69

3. Find the Answer—Mentally

Handout 1:
Basic Facts

TG page 110

Using an overhead projector, show a multiplication table you constructed with a student or the one provided on page 110, and point out that the first row and column illustrate the principle of 0 in multiplication. Also, show that the second row and column are identical to the row and column headings—1 is the **identity element** for multiplication.

When dealing with division, the importance of the order of the numbers makes both of these properties more complicated. Stress the examples that point out the importance of being careful.

PAGE 70

Building on Basic Facts

The estimation techniques introduced in this lesson are just the beginning steps of what will become a powerful way of thinking for your students. Students will probably not feel comfortable during this introductory phase, but by being persistent, you can help them feel "at home" with numbers. Building number sense is a major goal of this method of instruction. Along with competence in dealing with numbers, estimating helps students to develop enough confidence to be flexible in their thinking about mathematical problems.

PAGE 71

Calculator Exploration

Rather than tell students about the rules for divisibility, this exploration asks students to notice characteristic of numbers and then generalize the rules for themselves. The activity works on many levels, from interpreting a whole number answer as an indication of divisibility to recognizing the patterns that are present. Using the calculator's power to generate quick answers allows students to extend the basic facts and to gain a broader perspective.

The next activity also fosters the "big-picture" perspective that in turn may offer the insight that gives meaning to the smaller elements. It uses the divisibility rules that this exploration has generated and results in a chart that highlights the prime numbers.

EXTENSION ACTIVITY

Sieve of Eratosthenes

Handout 2:
Hundreds Chart

TG page 111

Before you begin this activity, define **prime numbers** (a number that can be evenly divided by only itself and 1) and **composite numbers** (a number that can be divided equally by other numbers as well). This activity will give students the most effective display of patterns formed by **multiples**.

Give each student a copy of the hundreds chart (TG page 111). Then instruct them to follow these steps to see the patterns that will be formed:

1. Start with the first row, omitting 1. One by one, analyze each number using the definition to see if it is prime or composite. Cross out the composites, and put boxes around the prime numbers up to 9. By the time you get to 9, you will want to be more efficient.

```
 1  [2] [3]  X  [5]  X  [7]  X   X  10
11  12  13  14  15  16  17  X   19  20
21  22  23  24  25  26  X   28  29  30
31  32  33  34  35  X   37  38  39  40
41  42  43  44  X   46  47  48  49  50
51  52  53  X   55  56  57  58  59  60
61  62  X   64  65  66  67  68  69  70
71  X   73  74  75  76  77  78  79  80
 X  82  83  84  85  86  87  88  89  X
91  92  93  94  95  96  97  98  X  100
```

2. With a black marker, cross out the multiples of 9. From the calculator exploration, students know the divisibility rule for 9; note that they form a diagonal across the page. (We started with the 9s so that the pattern would be apparent.)

3. Next, use a red marker to draw a line through the numbers that are divisible by 5. Students know that these will be in the columns with numbers ending in 5 and 0.

```
 1  [2] [3]  X  [5]  X  [7]  X   X  10
11  12  13  14  15  16  17  X   19  20
21  22  23  24  25  26  X   28  29  30
31  32  33  34  35  X   37  38  39  40
41  42  43  44  X   46  47  48  49  50
51  52  53  X   55  56  57  58  59  60
61  62  X   64  65  66  67  68  69  70
71  X   73  74  75  76  77  78  79  80
 X  82  83  84  85  86  87  88  89  X
91  92  93  94  95  96  97  98  X  100
```

4. Similarly, draw a green line through columns of numbers that are even—the multiples of 2. Analyze the results. How many even numbers are prime?

Note that we have not yet crossed out the composite numbers that are multiples of 3 or 7.

5. Start with 3. Put black **X**s on all the multiples of 3. Six is even, 9 is odd, 12 is even, 15 is odd, and so forth. When you are finished, you will note that these also form diagonal patterns. They also show that multiples of 3 are every third number. Again analyze the result and decide on the next step. Ask students, "Why don't you have to cross out any multiples of 4?" (They were all eliminated when you crossed out the multiples of 2.) "Are there any multiples of 6 that are not crossed out?" (No, the combination of multiples of 2 and 3 took care of all of them.)

```
 1  [2] [3]  X  [5]  X  [7]  X   X  10
11  X   13  14  X   16  17  X   19  20
 X  22  23  X   25  26  X   28  29  X
31  32  X   34  35  X   37  38  X   40
41  X   43  44  X   46  47  X   49  50
 X  52  53  X   55  56  X   58  59  X
61  62  X   64  65  X   67  68  X   70
71  X   73  74  X   76  77  X   79  80
 X  82  83  X   85  86  X   88  89  X
91  92  X   94  95  X   97  98  X  100
```

6. Ask students, "What is the first multiple of 7 that is not yet crossed out?" (It is 49 because smaller multiples were crossed out when you did the multiples of the smaller primes. For example, $35 = 5 \times 7$ was included in the multiples of 5.) You will also need to cross out 77 and 91. Using this same logic ask students, "Is it possible for any of the unmarked numbers to be composite numbers?" (No, the next prime number is 11, and $11 \times 11 = 121$.)

7. Put boxes around all the numbers that have not been crossed out. These are the prime numbers less than one hundred. Point out once more that a prime is a number that is not divisible by any number other than itself and 1. Familiarity with the prime numbers will add a new dimension to students' number sense.

PAGES 72–74

4. Check for Reasonableness

Again, estimating is emphasized as a method to tell whether or not a calculated answer is reasonable.

Rounding and Estimating

When estimating with multiplication, rounding one or both of the factors to the nearest hundred or thousand is a perfectly good first step in finding an approximate answer. The decision as to how much rounding to do is affected only by what the estimator is capable of doing mentally. However, with division, it is better to use more creativity in rounding. In **Problems 12** and **13**, students choose between rounding to the nearest 10, 100, or 1,000 to make the problem easier. These problems lead into finding compatible numbers for division.

In **Problem 13Ⓐ**, for example, instruct students to look at the denominator first. Ask, "Will 7 go into 4? Will 7 go into 41? In this problem, what number would you choose to divide 7 into?" Students should choose 42. The divisor determines how many non-zero digits of the numerator are needed in order to divide. The rest of the digits can be regarded as zeros and placed in the answer.

In **Problem 14**, students are asked to take one step further than simple rounding in determining a compatible number. In **Problem 14Ⓑ**, for example, students will use their knowledge of multiples to find the multiple of 8 that is nearest to 62. Don't expect that this idea will be easy for students to accept. However, it is an important one for establishing ideas of proportionality; it is reinforced and extended throughout the book.

PAGE 76

GED Practice

Problem 3 asks students to carry out a multistep problem. We have not discussed how to approach such problems in this book yet, but I've included this one here because I think that many of your students will be able to "puzzle it out." I think that it is important for students to realize, sooner rather than later, that they cannot expect all GED items to be simple exercises or a rephrasing of a question that they have seen before. By design, the test assesses the ability to transfer skills to unfamiliar situations.

EXTENSION ACTIVITY

Numeracy from the Newspaper (pairs and whole class)

To extend your discussion of **Problem 3**, refer to "The Price of Power" in the Appendix (page 293). This page of data comes from a newspaper article published during the energy crisis in California. Critical reading of documents that have mathematical content is an important element of numeracy for citizenship. The questions that follow apply to this article and can serve as a useful example, but you should bring similar articles from your local paper and discuss them from a mathematical perspective.

Instruct pairs of students to scan the page and look for any data that is surprising. Then focus on the last two columns. Ask which uses less electricity per hour, a radio or a 100-watt light bulb. Look for the apparent inconsistencies between the costs per day and the costs per month. (For small electric appliances, the monthly cost divided by the daily cost is 34, while for a light bulb the monthly cost divided by the daily cost is close to 29.) Ask students to come up with some plausible explanations for these inconsistencies. One explanation for the inconsistencies might be due to a rounding issue; rounding daily costs to the nearest cent or the nearest 10 cents. Check by dividing the monthly costs by 30. Ask students, "Would each result that you get be rounded to the daily figure that is printed?" There are some exceptions that could be errors.

If your students want to explore further, direct them to other power sites, http://www.nppd.com/customers/usage.asp, for example, to compare the figures that are given.

8 LESSON

Measurement: Multiplying More Than Two Numbers

OBJECTIVES

Students will

- use units of measure in both the English and metric systems
- recognize which attribute (length, area, or volume) is represented in a situation
- recognize the shapes and characteristics of a rectangle, parallelogram, and triangle
- multiply with more than two multipliers, using grouping of compatible factors to make it easier to find the answer mentally

Background

Geometrical figures and measurement (particularly the area of triangles and the volume of rectangular solids) provide the context for multiplying more than two numbers, another example of the power of integrating the mathematical strands.

Handout 8:
Centimeter Grid

TG page 117

Handout 9:
Polygons

TG page 118

A Hands-On Experience

This is a hands-on lesson. Do not allow this to become merely a lesson in finding formulas and substituting values in them. Experience shows that students need to manipulate the materials in order to make the applications of this subject relevant. The following materials and equipment are recommended to make this lesson real for students:

- Measuring tapes and rulers for English and metric systems
- Centimeter grids on transparencies (TG page 117)
- Cubic centimeter blocks and cubic inch blocks
- Envelopes containing precut shapes. Include triangles (two of which are identical), rectangles, parallelograms, trapezoids, and other polygons of four, five, and six sides. A sample of shapes that will fit the centimeter grid are drawn for you on TG page 118. Reproduce this page on card stock, if possible.

Lesson Recommendations

PAGE 77

Mental Math

These mental math exercises provide a review of the important rules for zero and one. Students often need reminders of these fundamental rules.

PAGES 77-78

Units of Measure

Each student should have the experience of measuring with both the English and metric systems. Using the measuring tapes from both systems, expand **Problem 1** so that the students also measure their height, hand span, and arm span using both measures. (You could find which people are *square*, that is, have arm spans that are equal to their heights.) An additional benefit of this exercise is that students will become aware of some personal references of measure that will always be available to them. For example, a yard or meter is often the distance from a person's nose to the fingertips of his or her outstretched arm; and if one's shoe is not a foot long, the distance from elbow to wrist may be close to a foot in length. Be certain that each student goes away from this exercise with at least one of these "personal measures."

Expand **Problem 2** by asking which metric unit would be used for each measurement. Answers: ❹ km, ❺ m, ❻ m², and ❼ m³.

PAGE 78

Area

Many people who take the GED Test make the mistake of using the perimeter formula for area and vice versa. This error indicates a true lack of understanding concerning the attributes of length, perimeter, area, and volume. Some students with learning difficulties will not understand what distinguishes one from the other unless they actually *feel* areas by rubbing their hands over something like the desktop and *feel* perimeter by running their fingers along the sharp edge around the desk. (Thanks to Mary Jane Schmitt of Massachusetts for this observation.)

Even though some of your students already know the formulas for area that are in this lesson, they should participate in the discovery approach to finding area. What is discovery for some will be reinforcement for others. The discovery of the easiest way to find the number of square units in any rectangle should not be difficult for students. We see so many rectangular arrays (egg cartons and calendars, for example) that it is natural to find the number of rows and the number in each row.

PAGES 78-79

Rectangles

Make the point that, since what you do naturally is the same as the mathematical formula, there is no reason to panic when you forget the formulas.

It is interesting to note that in the real-life situation described in **Problem 5**, the estimate of square footage is the one that gives some allowance for waste and would be more useful in buying tile. You might want to mention that some tile setters like to add a 10% to 20% waste allowance to their measurement.

Reasoning Activity

This activity visually connects the idea of divisibility and areas. There are many different rectangles whose area is 24, because 24 is a multiple of many numbers, but not 5. The last two questions start students thinking about common multiples; to be able to use either size glass block, the dimensions must be multiples of both 8 and 12. Juanita's puzzle can be solved by thinking first about 20, a common multiple of 4 and 5. Count by 20s, adding three to each one until you get to a multiple of 9.

Handout 8:
Centimeter Grid

TG page 117

Handout 9:
Polygons

TG page 118

EXTENSION ACTIVITY

Working with 4-Sided Figures   (small groups)

Give small groups of students envelopes of precut shapes found on TG page 118 and a transparency of the centimeter grid on TG page 117. Instruct students to take the **rectangles** out of the envelope. Ask them, "What is it about these shapes that makes them rectangular?" (Important characteristics to cover are number of sides (4), opposite sides are equal and parallel, and right angles.) Do the same for **parallelograms** (opposite sides are equal and parallel; all rectangles are also parallelograms) and **trapezoids** (only two sides are parallel and these two are not equal).

PAGES 80–81

Parallelograms

By following the procedure to visualize how a parallelogram is transformed to a rectangle, use the cutout shapes and transparent grids so your students can see that the formula for the area of parallelograms makes sense. Allow them to actually cut the parallelogram and rearrange the pieces to form a rectangle.

It is important for students to recognize that the height of a parallelogram is different from the length of the slanted side. (This will be true again for triangles.) Point out that the height is perpendicular to the side that they determine to be the base (not necessarily the bottom side) and may be measured outside the figure. (See **Problem 7❸**.)

Triangles

To make the connection between the formulas for triangles and parallelograms visual as well as symbolic, students should use two of the identical triangles from the envelope and place them side by side (with equivalent sides touching) on a transparent grid to form a parallelogram. Point out that the measure of the height and base of both are the same.

PAGE 82

Regrouping to Multiply

Because the operation of multiplication is both commutative and associative, you can rearrange and regroup factors so that multiplying them mentally is easier.

PAGE 83

Irregular Figures

Irregular figures are very likely to be represented on the GED Test, since they present a problem-solving situation as well as a test of geometry skills. Review with students the strategy of dividing the complex figure into smaller shapes for which they know how to find the area. The first example shows the addition of the one smaller area, while the second example shows that one area can also be subtracted to find the remaining area.

PAGE 84

Volume

Finding the volume of a rectangular container follows the same logical pattern as finding the area of a rectangle. The formula confirms the common sense method. It would be most instructive if you had a small box that you could fill exactly with layers of actual cubic-inch or cubic-centimeter blocks. Some of these instructional materials are available at parent/teacher stores or in instructional materials catalogs. A cooperative industrial arts class also can construct them easily.

Again we have the freedom of multiplying any two of the numbers first and then multiplying that product by the third number.

PAGE 85

Finding the Answer Mentally

The section on compatible numbers depends mathematically on the associative and commutative properties discussed earlier. Compatible factors are two numbers that can be multiplied mentally to get a "nice" number (one that is easy to work with). For example, any multiple of 5 multiplied by any multiple of 2 will result in a number divisible by 10, a nice number. This can be expanded to the special cases of 4 and 25, and 2 and 50. These mental gymnastics are not difficult to carry out when students understand the underlying principles. Encourage students to write the factors as suggested in the examples so that they don't lose track of them.

The section on doubling and halving is included here because of the formula for the area of a triangle. The technique of breaking the number up into its parts (expanded form) and then multiplying or dividing each part by 2 is introduced here almost intuitively. **Lesson 10** will review this technique, basing its steps on the distributive property.

Your students should be gaining a feeling of empowerment as they learn these techniques and become more comfortable with numbers. Encourage students to keep practicing mental techniques rather than to automatically reach for paper and pencil or a calculator.

GED Practice

Problem 4 requires the student to count the squares to find the base and height of the triangle before they can find the area.

Problem 5 can be solved a number of ways, but it is probably easiest if you see the sidewalk as the difference between the large and small rectangles. To make that idea real, you may have to use two rectangular cutouts. Start with the area of the larger one. Place the smaller one on top asking how much area is now covered. The visible area of the larger one is the difference between their areas.

Equivalent Equations: Multiplication and Division

OBJECTIVES

Using two of the most practical relationships in daily life, $d = rt$ and $c = nr$, students will

- visualize multiplication relationships, using both a table and a graph
- write equivalent equations involving multiplication and division
- solve problems using "fact families" or algebraic techniques
- translate problem situations into mathematical equations
- develop number sense about what happens when they multiply and divide both positive and negative numbers

Background

Using Rates

This lesson provides the foundation for the study of rates. In later lessons, this will lead to ratios, proportions, percents, and even fractions. A thorough understanding of the basic relationship is critical to further success. For this reason, the scope of this lesson is limited to analyzing how the inverse operations of multiplication and division are related in a few practical applications.

The lesson is structured so that powerful mathematical principles are drawn from the mathematics that students already know. Everyone knows that the more items you buy, the more you will pay and that the longer you drive, the further you will go, but they do not often recognize this as mathematics. The aim here is first to make students realize that there is mathematics in what they know and then to make the mathematics that they know more powerful. By making generalizations about their experience they transform it into principles that can be applied to other situations. In her article, Diana Coben offers more insight into the idea of transferability. See page 40 of *Adult Numeracy Development; Theory, Research, Practice*, edited by IddoGal, 2000, Hampton Press, Inc, NJ.

Lesson Recommendations

PAGES 88–89

Mental Math

These exercises review the mental math techniques from the previous lesson.

Finding Total Cost

Analyze the table about CDs. Discuss both columns and the relationship between them. (As the number of CDs increases by 1, the cost increases by $14.)

Problem 1Ⓐ requires students simply to supply a missing value. They could either add 14 to 56 or multiply 14 by 5 to find the cost of 5 CDs. This serves as a reminder that multiplication is repeated addition.

Problem 1Ⓑ and **1Ⓒ** use specifics to lead students to generalize the formula for total price. They have to multiply the number of CDs (n) by the price per item (r for rate).

Finally, **Problem 1Ⓓ** requires students to summarize what they have been doing. Taken one step at a time using a familiar situation, the mathematics involved is not difficult.

The graph on page 89 allows students to visualize what happens when they multiply with numbers greater than 1. As the number of CDs increases, the total cost increases. Of course, this is not news to anyone in the class, but linking the concrete to the abstract may be something foreign to students. Make this generalization to introduce students to this facet of mathematical thinking.

Unlike the informational graphs we studied earlier, the points in this graph correspond to the values in the table that were generated using a mathematical rule. It is no accident that they form a straight line; they are generated from a linear function.

Arrows inserted in the graph guide students to answer the questions and also to see that the graph pictures both multiplication and division. For example, in **Problem 2Ⓑ**, the total cost is given. By finding that value ($100) on the vertical axis, they can determine the approximate corresponding value on the horizontal axis (7). Correlate that action with the symbolic: they divided $100 by 14 to find that value. In **Problem 2Ⓓ**, make the step to the abstraction. Generalize: To find the number of CDs, divide the total cost by 14, the price per item.

PAGES 89–90

Finding Distance

The second example, which analyzes the relationship $d = rt$, follows the same structure as the total cost formula. It will be easier for the students to navigate through this one on their own.

PAGES 90–91

Writing Equivalent Equations Using "Fact Families"

The preceding pages in the student book intuitively explored the relationship between multiplication and division by relying on students' experience with concrete examples. This section formalizes that relationship analytically with numbers and variables. The triangle provides a visual interpretation, showing the relationship between the two multipliers on one level and the product on the other. While writing the equivalent forms, students see that the product of the multiplication is always the dividend in the division problem.

The exercises in **Problem 7** give purpose to the preceding ones. Just as with addition and subtraction, students will use the idea of inverse operations to solve multiplication and division equations.

After practicing equation manipulation (using numbers and then variables), students apply what they have learned to the two formulas discussed earlier. Finally, they are asked to apply these techniques to specific problem situations.

PAGE 92

Solving Multiplication and Division Equations

Two different ways to approach formula problems are outlined in the example on page 92. The first way substitutes known values into the basic formula. An equivalent equation is then written so that the unknown value is alone. The abstract mechanics of symbol manipulation involved with equations tells the student what he or she has to do to find the answer. The other approach recognizes that some students know they have to divide cost by rate. What students may not know is that they're using an equivalent form of the formula. Encourage these students to write the problems in equation format so that their insight is translated to symbols. This is another example of making the math that they know more powerful.

The presence of a "not enough information" problem in **Problem 10** will disturb some. It is meant to prevent students from getting into a rut about problem solving, thinking that all the problems in a set will follow the pattern of the examples above it.

PAGE 93

Rewriting Equations Using Algebraic Rules

The Multiplication Property of Equality, like the one for addition studied earlier, is one of the first topics of elementary algebra. By combining the concept that multiplication and division are inverse operations (one undoes the other) and the fact that what you do to one side of the equation also has to be done to the other, a formal, somewhat mechanical, strategy for isolating the variable is defined.

Students should compare the intermediate steps here to what they did with the fact families. The algebraic approach results in exactly the same expressions.

Students should be familiar with the algebraic process but will not be required to use it instead of the fact family method once they have completed this lesson.

PAGES 94–95

Analyzing Answers

These two pages ask students to learn some major principles of number and operations by analyzing the answers they get from a few well-constructed problems. The principles will expand their number sense, allowing them to make more accurate estimates and detect unreasonable answers that may appear on a calculator display. The problems also provide a basis for explaining the reasonableness of answers found when multiplying by a fraction in the next section.

By using the $C = nr$ relation again, students know the specifics—that you will pay more than $12 for 12 gallons of gas when the price per gallon is over a dollar. Build on their everyday knowledge, and point out the underlying mathematical principle. *Make your students more aware of the mathematics they already know.* In this case, students use this awareness to predict the size of answers before they multiply or divide.

Problems 13❶ and **16❺** represent the main concepts. You can give these more emphasis by providing further examples. The statements that are generated are true for positive numbers.

PAGES 96–97

Multiplying and Dividing with Negative Numbers

Use the fact that multiplication is repeated addition to make sense of the algebraic rule of multiplying a positive number by a negative number. The fact that a negative times a negative is a positive takes more creativity to explain. The need to continue the pattern in the table is a powerful explanation but may not satisfy everyone. One example that may strengthen the sense that the opposite of a negative is positive is illustrated by the action of removing a debt from one's statement of net worth.

I read this creative illustration on the Internet from an African math teacher:

> Consider good people to be positive (+) and bad people to be negative (−) and consider "moving in" to be positive (+) and "moving out" to be negative (−).
>
> Thus, good people moving in (+) (+) is positive (+),
>
> Good people moving out (+) (−) is negative (−),
>
> Bad people moving in (−) (+) is negative (−), and
>
> Bad people moving out (−) (−) is positive (+).

The division rules are derived using the ideas of equivalent equations. When written as equivalent multiplication equations, the division rules are obvious.

Equations and Problem Solving

This set of problems revisits the ideas of the lesson in a new situation. Graphs developed from points that make an equation true will reappear throughout the remainder of the book. Answers can be found using the table, the graph, or the equation. Make this one a group activity and listen to the variety of ways that the students explain their methods to one another. For example, how did students find the cost of 9 pounds of apples? Did they see the pattern in the table and provide the missing number, or did they find the cost per pound and multiply by 9? Did students estimate how many pounds they could buy from the graph, the table, or did they try to use an equation?

Multistep Problems

OBJECTIVES

Students will

- use the standard order of operations to find values of expressions with more than one operation
- recognize the order in which their calculator processes a series of operations and be able to circumvent it with parentheses
- multiply and factor using the distributive property
- recognize and combine like terms
- find the mean and median of a group of numbers and discern the effect of extremes in the data on each average
- write single equations describing the multiple steps needed to solve different problem situations

Background

Understanding and Recognizing Multistep Problems

The concepts introduced in this lesson (order of operations and the distributive property) are essential to the early study of algebra. For our purposes, they are more than rules that govern symbol manipulation; they are critical to discussions of multistep problems. They make up the "ground rules" that govern how multistep problems are written so that the order of the steps is conveyed.

Many of your students will have the experience and savvy to know how to use more than one step to solve real-life situations. For example, to figure how much change they should get from a $20 bill, they might add the prices of their purchases and then subtract that total from $20. They also are likely to have experience finding averages.

Build on the knowledge that they have and make it more powerful by teaching them how to recognize and write a single equation that combines the two steps. In a test situation, students may have to choose which listed equation says the same thing as their method. Beyond the test, this lesson could be critical in opening the doors to further study for students who have good problem-solving skills but shun the academic symbolic language of math. In the workplace as well, abstraction allows people to communicate their skills to others, a necessity for those who work as part of a team.

Lesson Recommendations

PAGE 100

Mental Math

These mental math exercises ask students to apply what they learned about multiplication and division. In multiplication, as the factors get greater, the answer increases. In **#1**, since 45 < 50, the answer to the second equation must be less than 3,750. However, in division, as the divisor increases, the answer decreases. In **#2**, since 95 < 100, the answer to the second equation must be greater than 57. Ask your students to verbalize the reasoning they used to determine their answer. For example, in **#2**, they might say that since 95 is less than 100, there are more of them in 5,700. This will help reinforce the concepts.

PAGES 100–101

Order of Operations

Have some fun with the example of 4 + 5 × 6. After establishing that two possible answers exist, debate their correctness and then suggest using a calculator as the arbiter. While a scientific calculator, such as the Casio *fx*-260 will have the order of operations built in, a simpler four-function calculator will not. Thus, the scientific calculator will give the answer of 34 while the simple one will display 54 as the answer. The fact that different calculators come up with different answers for the seemingly straightforward example of 4 + 5 × 6 makes students appreciate the need for a standard approach to the order of operations. (For this comparison, I use a simple calculator that was a gift from a bank when I opened an account with them. When it is shown to give the wrong answer, it becomes the butt of a few jokes.)

NOTE: The rules presented in this section are only part of the whole set of rules for the order of operations. The **P**lease **E**xcuse **M**y **D**ear **A**unt **S**ally rule will be introduced on page 117 after the introduction of exponents. In the meantime, the student text is very careful *not* to say to do the multiplications and divisions *first*. It says only to do them before the additions and subtractions. At the same time, note that the operation within the parentheses (or other grouping symbols) will always be completed first, even after exponents are discussed.

The interpretation of the fraction line as a grouping symbol is important in order to understand the formula for finding averages on the Formulas page of the GED Test.

PAGES 102–103

The Distributive Property

The Distributive Property is an important rule that guides symbol manipulation in algebra. Beyond using it to write expressions in two ways, we emphasize that it provides a basis for showing that two ways to find the answer are both correct. Take the time to explain to students how the areas of the rectangles on the top of page 102 represent both the *factored form* and the *expanded form*. The visual representation of the symbolic expressions will aid your students in accepting that the two statements produce the same answer.

Students practice the mechanics of converting from one form to the other so they can become comfortable doing it with constants and variables. On page 103, factoring out a common variable shows why combining "like" terms in algebra is possible. Practical examples where the distributive property is applied occur throughout the text. In addition to **Problem 5**, you can demonstrate its value for the GED Test by using the following example:

> Write an expression that shows the total distance traveled by a trucker who averages 55 miles per hour and travels 8 hours one day and 10 hours the next.

Some students may answer with $(55 \times 8) + (55 \times 10)$. While this is correct, they should be prepared to recognize the answer choice of $55(8 + 10)$ also is correct.

To summarize, the distributive property gives the choice of two ways to do the problem (it doesn't matter how it's done), but students must be able to recognize that both forms are equivalent.

PAGE 104

Calculator Exploration

The first two examples explain that to understand what a calculator is doing, students should watch the display as they enter a series of numbers and operation signs. They will see that the Casio *fx*-260 does multiply and divide before it adds or subtracts. (When the $\times$ sign is entered after $3 + 2$, the display continues to read $\boxed{2.}$. But when the $+$ sign is entered after 3×2, the display changes to $\boxed{6.}$.)

The calculator can be forced to follow a different order by inserting parentheses around the operation that is to be done first. The examples show that this would be necessary when the distributive property is being applied or when a fraction bar is used as a grouping symbol.

Frame the exercises as opportunities to judge in advance whether or not the grouping symbols (parentheses and fraction bars) in the problems are necessary.

PAGES 105–107

Use Formulas to Solve Real Problems

Two formulas provide practical examples of how the distributive property is applied to real situations. Both the perimeter of a rectangle and the mean (average) of a group of numbers are often represented on the GED Test and both formulas appear on the Formulas page, (page 280 in the student book). Students *can* begin with the formulas, substitute the known values in them, and mechanically find an answer. In both cases, however, the student book tries to make sense of the formulas so that problem solving involves critical thinking, rather than just substituting numbers into a formula. You can promote the reasoning aspect of the formula for the mean with the following activity.

Division and the Distributive Property (whole class)

Finding a mean can be an example of how the distributive property works for division as well as multiplication. When you find the average of two numbers, it is interesting to show that you can either add first and then divide by two, or divide each number by two and then add the results.

EXAMPLE Find the average of 56 and 42.

SOLUTION A		SOLUTION B	
1. Add first.	$56 + 42 = 98$	**1.** Divide first.	$56 \div 2 = 28$
			$42 \div 2 = 21$
2. Divide by 2.	$98 \div 2 = 49$	**2.** Add the results.	$28 + 21 = 49$

The median as another measure of central tendency is also discussed here. Comparing the two values, mean and median, gives students an appreciation for why there are two of them. In the two cases that are described in **Problems 8** and **9**, house prices and salaries, the median will be the measure that seems more typical of the group. Often we see that median is the measure of choice in cases like these when there is no upper limit on the values. Bring examples from the newspaper of instances where either or both of these measures is used. Introduce an element of skepticism as to why a particular organization uses one over the other.

Problems 9D and **9E** provide specific examples of how the two averages, mean and median, are affected by different changes in the group of numbers. If all numbers are changed, both the mean and median are also changed. However, if an outlier is changed, only the mean reflects that change.

Mean and Median (in pairs)

If your class needs a more visual and tactile lesson on mean and median, try this activity. It finds the average number of letters in the names of class members.

Cut 1-cm graph paper into strips and give 10 to 15 strips to each pair.

As a class, decide on 5 first names of people in the class to use and write them, one letter in each square, on 5 of the strips. Tear off the extra squares.

Arrange the names in order, from the least number of letters to the greatest, as illustrated in the following example:

T	O	M

J	E	N

R	A	U	L

L	U	P	E

R	O	B	E	R	T	A

Count the number of letters in each name and enter them in order on a separate strip of paper, one number in each square.

3	3	4	4	7

To find the **median**, simply fold the strip with the number of letters in half, end to end.

For an odd number of names, the median number is the number through which the fold passes. For an even number of names, the median is the number that is halfway between the two numbers on either side of the fold. In the example, the median is 4. (Finding the median is equivalent to finding the middle number when they are arranged in order.)

fold

3	3	4	4	7

To find the **mean**, try to balance the lengths of the strips with the names. Tear off letters from the longer names and connect them to the shorter names until all the names have as close to the same number of letters as possible. In the example, the mean is between 4 and 5. (Finding the mean is equivalent to finding how many letters would be in each name if they all were of equal length, or nearly so.)

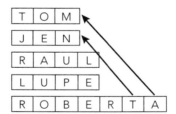

What if?

Play with the names several times. For example, you could make some change that lengthens one of the longer names. For instance, Lupe decides not to use her nickname. She uses Guadalupe instead. Now repeat the process and find the mean and median again. How did the change affect the two averages?

Translate a Situation into Mathematics—"Mathematize"

The rest of the chapter focuses on writing expressions that accurately reflect the mathematical processes that are needed to solve a real multistep problem. These do not follow a formula so are often more difficult for students. For this reason, the text begins with simple word phrases to translate into mathematics before looking at situations described in word problems. Before you go on to discuss the problems, you may want to take time to review *when* to add (combining unlike amounts), multiply (combining equal quantities), subtract (separating or comparing), or divide (separating into equal groups).

Ask students to interpret the problem situation first as a combination of operations. Allow time for them to figure things out. The middle step (how to plan it) shown in the examples tries to emphasize that, in complicated cases, one must do a great deal of planning before writing an equation. Unfortunately, the static nature of a page in a book does not convey the fact that much discussion might be necessary before a plan is formed or an equation is written.

When you do **Problems 12** and **13** together, have the class discuss general approaches. Then each student should individually try to write an equation for each problem. Ask students to share these equations for class discussion. Let the class discuss and judge whether or not the different equations are equivalent to the one given in the answer.

With this exercise, you are building your students' skills in recognizing the correct answer in a set-up problem on the test. You are also teaching them to respect methods of solution other than their own. Moreover, the class discussion allows everyone to learn from each other's mistakes. If the students don't come up with an incorrect equation, you should introduce a few. Maintain an atmosphere where mistakes are welcomed as learning opportunities and are corrected without censure. Incorrect responses usually contain some element of correct reasoning that can be praised.

EXTENSION ACTIVITY

Another Way to Multiply: The Front-End Method

Page 299 in the student Appendix offers students an alternate way to compute the exact answer of a multiplication problem. You can introduce this method during **Lesson 10** as an example of the distributive property and why it works. This method, called the front-end method, relies heavily on students' ability to handle trailing zeros (see page 70 of the student book). The features that follow are what I like about this method.

1. The first partial product is a good estimate of the answer.

2. The rectangular diagrams help students to picture the process. For many adult students, being able to "see" a process is necessary for learning. This method is easier to visualize than the traditional procedure.

3. It has fewer rules than the traditional multiplication algorithm. For example, when multiplying two 2-digit numbers, the order in which you multiply is not important as long as you multiply each digit of one number by each digit of the other number.

Some may view this method as being less efficient than the traditional algorithm because it takes up more lines. I personally feel this is a small sacrifice to pay for a method that emphasizes understanding of the process involved. Another reference to this method occurs in **Lesson 13** when we review the estimation technique for multiplying.

PAGE 111

GED Practice

Problem 2 asks students to follow the steps that an unfamiliar formula dictates. They know the notations, so many should be able to succeed. Being able to understand what a formula is telling you to do, even though you may not understand why, is a survival skill that is sometimes referred to derisively as "plug and chug."

Powers and Roots

OBJECTIVES

Students will

- use the notation of exponents and evaluate expressions containing exponents
- use the $\sqrt{}$ sign and recognize finding the square root as the inverse operation of squaring
- expand the standard order of operations to include exponents and radicals
- reverse the order of operations when solving multistep algebraic equations
- estimate the square root of numbers that are not perfect squares
- apply the Pythagorean theorem to find the length of a side of a right triangle
- apply the related concepts of squaring and finding square roots to the areas of squares and circles

Background

The mystery surrounding the exponent and the radical sign has traditionally made this topic seem like a foreign language to students. However, once the notation of exponents is understood, solving problems with them is easy. This lesson makes the notation understandable, makes the student comfortable with squares and square roots, and then applies both operations in formulas involving geometric figures.

Lesson Recommendations

PAGES 114–115

Mental Math

The topics of squaring numbers and finding square roots are introduced through the operations of multiplication and division.

Exponents

The operation of raising a number to a power is introduced as a shorter way to multiply identical factors, just as multiplication was introduced as a shorter way to add identical addends.

Students often confuse problems like 3^2 with $3 \cdot 2$. Help them to differentiate multiplying factors and raising a number to a power through a compare and contrast activity. For example, show pairs of problems like $4^3 = ?$ and $4 \times 3 = ?$, and ask students to explain the thinking that led to their answers.

Problem 1 illustrates four ways to write or say exponential values. Use the x^y key on the calculator to find the final values.

PAGES 115–117

Squares

The first and most obvious application of exponents is in finding the area of a square. Tell students that it is no accident that the operation and the shape have the same name. The second example illustrates the reasoning behind the conversion from square feet to square inches. Similar reasoning is expected of the student in the Reasoning Activity that follows.

Reasoning Activity

Handout 8:
Centimeter Grid

TG page 117

This activity works best with small groups. Each group should have a page of the 1-cm grid paper (TG page 117) for this activity.

The diagram should give visual verification first, that there are 3^2, or 9 square feet in a square yard, and second, that there are two possible ways to make the conversion from one to the other. In part **D**, students can either first divide the lengths of the sides by 3 and then multiply, or they can multiply first and then divide by 9. For part **E**, only one method, dividing the number of square feet by 9, is practical.

Square Roots

Use a variety of approaches, visual, verbal, and symbolic, to explore the inverse relationship between squaring and finding the square root. Visually, finding $\sqrt{16}$ can be pictured by a square of 16 square units reducing to a line of 4 units. Verbally, repeat the question "What number multiplied by itself is 16?" and use the word *unsquare* parenthetically for a time until the students really accept the words *find the square root*.

Symbolically, writing the equivalent equations in **Problem 4** is a critical step in solving simple algebraic equations involving squares. Give more practice with examples like these:

Write $3^2 = 9$ and expect students to respond with $\sqrt{9} = 3$.

Write $\sqrt{100} = 10$ and expect them to reply $10^2 = 100$.

Write $25 = x^2$ and expect them to reply with $x = \sqrt{25}$.

PAGES 117–119

Order of Operations

With the introduction of exponents and radicals, you now have the full spectrum of operations and can formalize the rules for order of operations in the standard format. We have merely inserted the exponents between the parentheses and the operations of multiplication and division. Take time with **Problem 6**. The similar structure of the problems calls attention to the differences that are important. They are designed to help you diagnose any misunderstandings that still remain.

The order of operations involved when solving an algebraic equation is just the opposite of that involved when simplifying an expression. **Problem 8** consists of equations that can be solved in two steps, adding or subtracting and then dividing. Expand the operations to include finding the square root by "undoing" some of the examples in **Problem 7**. For example, start with the equation $3x^2 = 75$. The principle remains the same: "undo" in the opposite order than when you "did." In this case, divide both sides by 3 first, then find the positive square root of both sides to end with $x = 5$.

PAGES 119–121

Pythagorean Theorem

Most questions on the non-calculator half of the GED Test that use the Pythagorean theorem will likely involve a Pythagorean triple—whole numbers that fit the relationship. Therefore, the discussion in the student book begins with a definition of the theorem, and then talks about these special groups of numbers that "work" nicely into the formula. Many are multiples of 3, 4, and 5.

To explore beyond the Pythagorean triples as possible sides of a right triangle, go to the Website, www.arcytech.org/java/pythagoras/index/html. Under Tip #1, there is a triangle that you can manipulate, adjusting the lengths of the sides with the mouse while the measures of the lengths are displayed on the side. For right triangles, students can try to manipulate the lengths to be equal to the Pythagorean triples they have learned. Under Tip #5, the sum of the squares of the legs is compared to the square of the hypotenuse in real time while you adjust the lengths of the sides. Students will see that as long as it is a right triangle, these two amounts will stay equal. (This same capability is available using a number of geometry software programs and even on some graphing calculators.)

NOTE: Your students may be interested to know that even before Pythagoras proved the theorem, builders in ancient times used its principle. A standard "tool" they carried was a length of rope, knotted at intervals corresponding to the lengths of 3, 4, and 5. They would use this to test whether or not the beams they were erecting were perpendicular.

PAGES 121–123

Estimating and Calculating Square Roots

The table of squares given in the student book is only a partial table showing some of the squares that are helpful in estimating square roots. Knowing benchmarks like these makes it easier to judge the reasonableness of answers. To aid students, remind them what they already know.

1. Students know the squares of the numbers 1 through 12 from the multiplication facts.

2. Students can find the squares of numbers such as 20 by using what they've learned about trailing 0s. For example, $20 \times 20 = 400$.

3. Encourage students to memorize special cases such as 15^2 and 25^2.

The text accompanying the table explains its use in estimating square roots of numbers that are not perfect squares. This process of finding a value between those given in a table is called **interpolation**, an important skill in itself.

Today, most people use a calculator to find the square root of a number. On the Casio *fx*-260, use the **SHIFT** key and the **x²** key to access the square root function. Students can practice using the square root function to check their answers to the questions in **Problem 12**.

Students are expected to use a calculator for **Problems 14–16**.

EXTENSION ACTIVITY

Consecutive Squares

(in pairs)

This activity shows the relationship between consecutive perfect squares. Students will benefit both from the extra exposure to perfect squares and from the practice they get in recognizing a pattern from a table of numbers. First, list only the numbers and their squares in a table. You might ask for general observations about the table, for instance, that as the numbers increase, the squares are further from

number	square
1	1 +3
2	4 +5
3	9 +7
4	16 +9
5	25 +11
6	36 +13

each other. Ask students to look for some pattern in the column of squares that would help to predict the next square. You may have to give some hints or even help students get started with the first few squares.

Have students explore whether or not the pattern found in the first six squares will continue. Instruct one person in each pair to continue the adding process with numbers up to 20 and the other person to simultaneously find the squares by using the calculator.

NOTE: Explain to students that the difference between consecutive squares is always odd. If one square is even, the next will be odd. See if your students know why. (Multiplying an odd number times an odd number always results in an odd number, and an even number times any number always results in an even number.)

Patterns with Squares

(in pairs)

This activity shows students the interesting patterns formed by the last digits of perfect squares. Students can use the table they made in the previous activity for this one as well. Focus only on the last digit of each perfect square.

What digits can be the last digit of a perfect square?

$0^2 = \boxed{0}$ 0
$1^2 = \boxed{1}$ 1
$2^2 = \boxed{4}$ 4
$3^2 = \boxed{9}$ 9
$4^2 = 1\boxed{6}$ 6
$5^2 = 2\boxed{5}$ 5
$6^2 = 3\boxed{6}$ 6
$7^2 = 4\boxed{9}$ 9
$8^2 = 6\boxed{4}$ 4
$9^2 = 8\boxed{1}$ 1
$10^2 = 10\boxed{0}$ 0

Notice that the last digits in the answers are **palindromic**. (They read the same backward and forward.)

Ask students, "Does the pattern continue through the entire table?" (Yes.) "Do any of the perfect squares having two or more digits have all odd digits?" (No.) "Do any have all even digits?" (Yes, 20 × 20 = 400.)

PAGE 124

Check Your Understanding

Problems 9 and **10** introduce the formula for finding one's Body Mass Index (BMI). After they have found the answers using the formula, refer to the table on page 286 of the Appendix. They should use the chart to verify that their answers using the formula are similar to what the table would give. Expect to see slight differences due to rounding.

The formula for finding one's BMI using metric measures is similar. The formula is BMI = $\frac{W}{H^2}$, where W is the weight in kilograms and H is the height in meters. Tell students to find the corresponding metric measures (from the table) to those used in **Problems 8** and **9** and then use the metric formula. Ask, "Do you get the same answers? If not, where is the error? Is it in the equivalencies implied by the chart or in the formulas themselves?"

(If you use the standard equivalencies of 1 meter = 39.37 inches and 1 kilogram = 2.2 pounds, you will find that 70 inches = 1.78 meters, not 1.75 meters as implied by the table. If you use 100 kilograms and 1.78 meters in the metric formula, the BMI is exactly the same as the result using the customary units and its formula. This leads us to conclude that the two formulas are equivalent but the table that combines the two systems of measurement is a little off.)

Your students may be getting a little skeptical of the accuracy of published tables and charts. Discuss the purpose of visual representations of data. Visual representations are meant to be an easier and more dramatic way to tell the story that the data reveals. For the most part, they do a good job of showing the big picture. However, to fit the constraints of table and chart construction, precision is often sacrificed. If accuracy is demanded, go to the mathematics that underlies the charts.

Circles

OBJECTIVES

Students will

- use the special vocabulary of circles
- use various approximations for the value of π
- find the circumference and area of a circle when given either the radius or the diameter
- find the radius or diameter when given the circumference or area of a circle
- discriminate between problem situations that involve area and those that involve circumference

Background

Understanding Circles

Circles, along with the strange number π, create stumbling blocks for many adult basic math students. For that reason, this entire lesson is devoted to circles.

Make this a hands-on lesson to minimize the mystery surrounding circles. Once students actually experience the fact that a circle's circumference is a little more than 3 times its diameter, they will not forget it, nor will they be stymied by the value of π.

Lesson Recommendations

PAGES 126–127 ## Mental Math

These exercises provide a quick review of the meaning of the radical sign.

Radius and Diameter

What is a circle? Precisely speaking, a circle consists only of the curved line and not the enclosed area. The actual definition of the circumference is "the length of a circle." The same principle applies to a rectangle and its perimeter. Realistic models of these shapes would be made of bent wire or plastic drinking straws rather than pieces of cardboard.

Circumference and Pi (π)

Emphasize that the fact that the ratio between the circumference and diameter of any size circle is always the same number came first and forced mathematicians to investigate that number. Also be careful to refer to the various approximations of π as just that—approximations. Students seem to think of 3.14 as a *precise* value for π. All of the computations of the circumference of circles are *approximations*; those using 3.14 are merely closer than those done with 3, and those using the π key on the calculator are even more accurate than those done with 3.14.

If the technology is available, encourage students to research the topic of pi on the Internet. They will find that it occupied the attention of mathematicians in many countries for centuries and that, even recently, entire books have been written about it.

Calculator Exploration

This activity works best with small groups. Students should experience for themselves where the value of π comes from. To get some level of reliability, each object should be measured by at least two groups of students.

1. Stretch the measuring tape out on the table or floor. (You may want to tape it down.) Make a mark on the edge of each object to serve as both the starting and ending point. Carefully line up the starting point on the object with the zero mark on the tape. Roll the circular object along the tape stopping when the mark touches the tape again. Record the length of the circumference of each object. (**NOTE:** For some objects it may be easier to wrap a piece of masking tape around the objects, making a mark where it overlaps, and then removing the tape to measure.)

2. Remind students that the diameter is the longest distance across the circle. Record the length of the diameter of each object.

3. Each group should use a calculator to find the ratio between the two measurements that they found. No matter what the size of the circle was, going around the circle took a little more than three of its diameters. This is remarkable. In fact, there were ancient cultures that worshiped the circle because of this "mysterious" property.

4. Use questions **Ⓐ**, **Ⓑ**, and **Ⓒ** to discuss students' findings.

Using Equivalent Equations

The previous activity showed the rearrangement of the formula $C = \pi d$ into $\frac{C}{d} = \pi$. A more useful arrangement of the formula in the real world is $d = \frac{C}{\pi}$. By using this form of the formula, you can find diameters that are difficult to measure.

PAGES 130–131

Area

The series of sketches on page 130 is certainly not a *proof* of the formula. (In the fourth picture, the circumference halves are pulled out to be straight lines. This would only be possible if the wedges were infinitely small.) This portrayal does, however, give some visual reference for what is likely a misunderstood concept. As you follow the sequence of pictures, focus attention on the fact that the radius is multiplied by itself. Multiplying one dimension by another is a common feature whenever you find area (two-dimensional). This point will help students to distinguish between finding area and finding the circumference of a circle.

Reasoning Activity

A circle is the shape that encloses the greatest area with a given length of perimeter or circumference. Students discover this fact by carrying out the calculations in this activity. It could be a factor in the shape of enclosures for cattle grazing. Extended to packaging options in three dimensions, a cylindrical can holds more than a square one with the same amount of surface so it minimizes the amount of tin that is required. A cylindrical electrical wire maximizes conductivity for a given surface.

EXTENSION ACTIVITY

Discovering a Formula for Volume (whole class)

Challenge your students to use what they have learned about circles and about volume to "invent" the formula for the volume of a cylinder. Place a cylindrical container next to a rectangular box. Ask students to remember what they did to find the volume of the box. They found the area of the bottom (number of cubes in the first layer), then multiplied by the height (number of layers). Follow the same sequence with the cylinder. The area of the bottom (a circle) is πr^2, and the height is h.

Check with the Formulas page to assure everyone that the formula is indeed $V = \pi r^2 h$.

Check Your Understanding

Problems 4 and **5** will be challenging for your students. You will need to discuss these problems together as a class. Give individuals an opportunity to spend time with the problems and figure them out by themselves before you intercede with any hints. For **Problem 4**, the fact that the radius is squared in the area formula will mean that the area is quadrupled when the radius is doubled. For **Problem 5**, you might want to ask for predictions before the calculations are done.

Problem 8 offers another possibility for an extended activity. Invite students to bring to class the prices of various sizes of pizzas sold at several local pizzerias. (They probably never realized that 12-inch, 14-inch, and so on referred to the diameter of the pizza.) Have students figure which size pizza gives the best value per square inch (area). They can also see which size gives the most circumference for the dollar.

More Powers – Powers of Ten

OBJECTIVES

By understanding the decimal system, students will

- write numbers in expanded form
- multiply and divide by powers of 10 by moving the decimal point
- write numbers, large and small, using scientific notation
- see the basis for their estimation techniques using multiplication and division and extend the techniques to include large numbers

Background

Putting It Together

The broad purpose of this lesson is to build number sense. Students will study the basics of place value through the manipulations of scientific notation and will review and standardize their estimation techniques. Emphasize how the laws of exponents and the concepts of place value in our system of numeration provide the reason why they can use the shortcuts they learned earlier. The lesson is a timely summary before Test-Taking Tips (**Lesson 14**).

Lesson Recommendations

PAGE 134

Mental Math

The ease of multiplying by powers of 10 is a result of having a number system based on 10. In this lesson, adding the trailing zeros will be correlated to moving the decimal point.

PAGES 134–136

Powers of 10 and Place Value

Students have intuitively used the idea of expanded numbers in previous lessons. Here it is stated explicitly: The value of a digit depends on the place it occupies.

One concept that may seem strange to students is that the ones place is designated as 10° in exponential form. As long as a is a non-zero number, $a^\circ = 1$.

Handout 4:
Place-Value Chart

TG page 113

Place Value and Exponents   (individual or small groups)

This activity is inserted here for you to use with students who have demonstrated a weakness with the ideas of place value as they have appeared in earlier lessons. In some cases, you may want to intervene at a "teachable moment" with this place-value chart. With other students, you may want to wait until this lesson. In either case, you are likely to be discussing the place value chart with only one individual or a small group. Either make a transparency of the full-page place-value chart (TG page 113) and use erasable markers, or just use a transparent overlay over a paper copy to write digits in the slots. Ask students to read the resulting numbers aloud.

EXAMPLE: Write a 7 in the thousands slot and a 5 in the tens slot. Read this number (seven thousand, fifty). Now move these same two digits, putting the 7 in the millions place and the 5 in the ten thousands place. Again read the resulting number (seven million, fifty thousand). Continue practicing until the student is comfortable with the place names.

In **Problems 1** and **2**, students make observations connecting the number of places between a digit and the decimal point to the number that is the exponent in the power of 10 that names that place. Since the students have done this kind of observing and recognizing patterns throughout the previous lessons, they should breeze through these. The observations are important, but the process of making them should also be emphasized as a critical facet of mathematical thinking.

PAGES 136–137

Multiplying and Dividing a Number by a Power of 10

Again use the full-page place-value transparency (TG page 113) to illustrate the examples. Write the number 49 on an *overlay* transparency, positioning the digits so that the 4 is on top of the 10s slot and the 9 is on top of the 1s slot. When 49 is multiplied by 100 using the mental technique of tacking on the trailing zeros, the result is 4,900. Show this by merely *sliding* your overlay over until the 4 is in the 1,000s slot. Use the same technique for the other three examples as well. It will dramatize how easy these problems are to solve and will provide a better sense of what moving the decimal point is all about.

Negative exponents will be new to most students. They can be interpreted using examples along with this phrase, "Multiplying by a number with a negative exponent is the same as dividing by that same number with a positive exponent."

EXAMPLE

4×10^{-3} is the same as $4 \div 10^3$ or $4 \div 1,000$ which is 0.004.
A similar way to look at it uses fractions.

4×10^{-3} is the same as $4 \times \frac{1}{10^3}$ or $4 \times \frac{1}{1,000}$ which is $\frac{4}{1,000}$.

PAGES 137–138

Scientific Notation

The topic of scientific notation as a shorthand way to write large and small numerical values is important for general numeracy. As a nation, we are accused of not realizing the difference between millions, billions, and trillions as we hear these astronomical figures describing the cost of programs and the budget deficit. The following statements are a dramatic introduction to stimulate students' thinking about the relative sizes of large numbers.

If you spent $1,000 a day, it would take about 3 years to spend $1 million. At that same rate ($1,000 a day), it would take you about 3,000 years to spend $1 billion.

The Casio *fx*-260 calculator can serve as a good motivator to study scientific notation. Enter 800,000 × 1,000,000 and press the ■ key. The answer has more digits than the screen can display so the calculator uses scientific notation to write the answer. The display will read $\boxed{8.^{11}}$, meaning 8×10^{11}. Similarly with small numerical values, enter 0.000005 × 0.000000003 and press the ■ key. The display will read, $\boxed{1.5^{-14}}$, meaning 1.5×10^{-14}. Students must be able to translate these displays into a numeral written in long form.

In most textbooks, the instructions to convert numerals from scientific notation to the long form and then back again will rely only on directional descriptions for moving the decimal point "to the left" or "to the right." Students will not remember which way to go if they do not have a sense of what kind of answer to expect. It is easy to recognize that a positive exponent in scientific notation corresponds to a large numerical value, while a negative exponent indicates a small value. Kept in mind, those ideas alone will dictate which direction the decimal point is moved.

PAGES 138–139

Estimating with Multiplication and Division

Combining scientific notation with the properties of exponents provides solid mathematical grounding for the techniques of tacking on or canceling common trailing zeroes that students used earlier. It also gives a convenient structure to the estimating process when large numbers are involved.

Problems 11, 12, and **13** are based on stories that appeared in the news while I was writing this chapter. You should be able to bring in some similar but timelier examples when you teach this lesson. It is a great motivational tool to investigate the mathematics behind the issues that affect students' lives.

PAGE 140

Using Data

Geographical data often involve large numbers and offer a perfect scenario to integrate mathematics and social studies. Here students are challenged to make the bar graph that would show the population distribution for different areas of the world. Deciding on the scale for the vertical axis is a very important step for groups of students to work out for themselves. Then, using the methods of this chapter, they convert data from the table in the Appendix to scientific notation so that they can determine the approximate density of the population in the various areas.

PAGE 141

Problem Solving with Multiplication and Division

This page ends the lesson and the chapter on multiplication and division with a summary of the kinds of situations that can be solved with those operations. It provides a good segue into the test-taking tips lesson that follows.

Many of your students will be happy to learn an alternate way to perform long division. The algorithm that is demonstrated on page 300 of the Appendix is commonly taught in many foreign countries. In trials in the United States, it has been found to be more "learner-friendly" than the method we learned traditionally. Skill in this technique increases as one's estimation powers increase. For this reason, it seems to be a natural method to use in this course which emphasizes estimation.

The student who is comfortable with the traditional algorithm for long division may notice that the last example corresponds closely to what he or she has mastered as a technique. This solution represents the highest estimation skills at work. It also points out the beauty of this method of instruction: One does not have to attain this level of efficiency in order to get the right answer.

PAGE 143

GED Practice

Problems 1 and **3** require the student to recognize the significance of the values that are listed on the vertical axis. Each numerical answer that is generated from the scale must be multiplied by 1,000 to answer the question. These two problems serve as a caution to students (and test-takers) to read the legends and titles of graphs carefully.

Test-Taking Tips

OBJECTIVES

Students will

- review the methods of this unit
- become familiar with some of the formats used on the GED Test
- evaluate their progress

Lesson Recommendations

To simulate the actual time allotted on the test, allow only 35–40 minutes for students to complete the test questions. Use the extra class time to review and redo problems that were troublesome for your class throughout this unit.

PAGES 144–145

Test-Taking Tips

Go over the examples on page 145 involving Art's Quik Lube. Students will see how the problem-solving process requires that they *apply* the basics that they know to new situations that may be unfamiliar. They will also be reminded of the insufficient-information problems, as well as the ones with extraneous information.

PAGES 146–149

Check Your Skills

When the students have completed the items in Check Your Skills, discuss the problems and possible solution strategies as you did for the first Test-Taking Tips (**Lesson 6**). Encourage students to reveal their personal methods of choosing the answer. Unorthodox methods should be accepted as long as you can see elements of correct mathematical thinking in the strategy.

As you go through the items, one by one, keep students alert by asking, "What different question could have been asked about this situation?"

For example, in **Problem 6**, the question could have asked for area.

For **Problem 13**, the question could have asked the total amount deducted from Richard's paychecks during the entire year.

For **Problem 19**, what if the two angles had been labeled $5x$ and $4x$ or $2x$ and $2x + 20$?

For **Problem 20**, can students find the mean for the data?

For those items where the method of solution was the final answer, ask students to carry out the procedure to find the answer that would be correct if the question were asked differently. In a test situation, they can use the fact that the answer is reasonable for the problem situation as an additional factor in determining which expression to choose.

Notice that the difficulty level of these items is closer to what students can expect to see on the GED Test. Most of the questions require more than one step to solve and many demand conceptual understanding beyond what is required for purely procedural problems. There are 5 questions on which the calculator was not allowed. They serve to indicate again that GED graduates are expected to be able to carry out computations and estimations with simple numbers.

At this point, most students should know the addition, subtraction, multiplication, and division facts well enough to enjoy the following game. You could arrange for others to follow along with a calculator in hand.

EXTENSION ACTIVITY

"I Have, Who Has?" Review   (whole class)

I learned this game, called "I Have, Who Has?" at an adult educator's workshop in Oklahoma. The game can be modified to review any math skills with any number of people participating. The sample shows 10 participants reviewing the skills we have studied.

MATERIALS: A set of 10 index cards, each containing one of these statements:

I have 10.	Who has the square of this?
I have 100.	Who has half as much?
I have 50.	Who has this, divided by 5, plus 2?
I have 12.	Who has double this?
I have 24.	Who has double this?
I have 48.	Who has this divided by 6?
I have 8.	Who has the square of this?
I have 64.	Who has this plus 6?
I have 70.	Who has this plus 20?
I have 90.	Who has this divided by 9?

As you construct sets of cards to fit your class and what you are doing, keep in mind these restrictions: First, no number can be repeated as an answer. Second, the series of questions should be circular, ending at the same number where it started. Ideally, there will be one card per person.

PROCEDURE: Shuffle the cards and pass them out, one to each person. Start with anyone. Have that student read his or her card aloud clearly. The person whose number satisfies the question responds by reading his or her card. The next one responds in turn until the process ends back at the starting person. Everyone must remain alert and continue to compute mentally to be able to recognize his or her number when it is described.

MODIFICATIONS: You should have several sets of cards on hand. The subject matter can fit what you have just studied, or it can provide a review. After seeing the pattern, some students may want to construct their own set for the class.

If the topic is purely review, you can make this game more challenging by giving each student two or more cards.

Size of Fractions

OBJECTIVES

Students will develop number sense about fractions by being able to

- understand the meaning of a fraction, not only as part of a whole, but also simply as a division problem
- recognize which fractions have values close to 1 and $\frac{1}{2}$
- rename fractions, whose numerators are greater than their denominators, as mixed numbers
- interchange common fractions with their decimal equivalents
- recognize equivalent fractions intuitively when working with rulers, and analytically, using mathematical principles
- apply fractions in expressing the probability of events occurring and in denoting parts of units of measurement
- use the a b/c key on the calculator to convert common fractions and mixed numbers to decimals and vice versa

Background

A Different Approach to Fractions

Neither the emphasis nor the methods of this group of lessons on fractions follow the traditional textbooks. There are two reasons for this. First, fractions are becoming less important in problems that occur in everyday life. Now that more calculating is being done by machines, more numbers are expressed in decimal form rather than in fraction form. Second, the old way did not work very well. Students did not understand why the procedures worked and soon forgot which of the manipulation rules to use when. They became more adept at avoiding fractions than at understanding them.

In this book, students will be taught to carry out the operations with the common fractions that occur frequently in measurement situations. With fractions that are less common and more difficult to picture, they will be taught to estimate.

This particular lesson focuses on understanding the concept of a fraction and its size. The transition from whole number operations to fractions is made less abrupt by the discussion of the value of a fraction as being the answer to the division problem that it represents. Equivalent fractions are introduced and the relative size of fractions is discussed intuitively and is demonstrated by reading a ruler. In later lessons, these topics will become the foundation for the estimation procedure and an intuitive understanding of the operations with fractions.

You may want to use a series of short answer questions as an introduction to fractions. Ask your students to write answers to these questions:

1. Which of these numbers has the least value, $\frac{1}{8}$, –8, or 0? Which number has the greatest value?

2. What is the relationship between fractions and decimals?

3. Write a mathematical expression for three tenths.

Don't discuss the answers at this time. Collect the papers and explain that you will return them after you ask the same questions after they study this section. Students will be able to see the evolution of their conceptual development and note their progress.

Lesson Recommendations

PAGE 150

Mental Math

These mental math exercises help students review how the size of the divisor (about to be discussed as the denominator) affects the answer.

PAGES 151–153

What Does a Fraction Mean?

The idea that a fraction is a part of a whole is an important one for visualizing what is going on when operating with fractions. However, the interpretation of a fraction as a division problem is the one that connects what students already know (division of whole numbers) with the meaning of fractions. Students should be reassured to find that these dreaded fractions are just another way to write a division problem and that the value of a fraction is merely the answer to the division problem (numerator divided by denominator).

Review the fact that the order of numbers in a division problem makes a difference. The problem $\frac{4}{5}$ is different from $\frac{5}{4}$. Use the same words you used with division to determine the decimal value of $\frac{4}{5}$. For example, you could think of the problem as 4 divided by 5, the number of 5s in 4, or a lesser number divided by a greater number. All should lead logically to an answer less than 1. Similarly, for $\frac{5}{4}$, students should expect a value greater than 1.

The term *improper fraction* is not used in this book to describe fractions with values greater than 1. The term carries a negative connotation that is not appropriate in most cases. While mixed number notation is often easier to use when comparing their sizes, there is no mathematical reason to require that values greater than one be written as mixed numbers. In fact, they are often easier to work with when they are expressed as single fractions. In algebra classes, students are expected to leave answers as single fractions instead of mixed numbers.

Plotting the values of the fractions on the number line in **Problem 1** is an important learning activity because it connects fractions with previous learning. I have seen that students often have serious misconceptions about the value of fractions. As an introductory question to the topic of fractions in my classes, I often asked students to place $\frac{2}{3}$ on a number line that extended from –3 to 3. Most put it between 2 and 3, many thought it should be less than 0, and only a few located it between 0 and 1.

PAGES 153–155

Comparing Fractions

The diagrams of fractions as part of a whole and the reference to fractional parts of a dollar are designed to make students feel more at ease with fractions and ultimately to give them more options when they are estimating with fractions. Emphasize that, while they can always use their calculators (and the decimal equivalents) to find out precisely which fraction is greater, reasoning it out mentally is often much easier and helps them to refine their number sense about fractions.

The underlying principle used to compare the values of fractions with the same denominator is precisely the same as that used to compare the size of decimal fractions in **Lesson 2**. Once the decimals had the same number of decimal places (the same denominator), the students focused only on the numerators.

Students should begin the process of committing the fraction and decimal equivalents to memory. Just as you did when they were memorizing the basic facts of addition and multiplication, you need to emphasize the meaning that underlies the equivalencies. Begin by reminding students how much they already know because of their familiarity with money. Point out the connections between the equivalents and encourage students to develop ways to reason them out if they forget them. Reinforce these equivalencies whenever possible.

EXTENSION ACTIVITY

Fractions from Random Numbers   (in pairs)

Ask students to create fractions from random numbers that are generated by tossing a 10-sided die. (These are available from education supply companies; the 10 faces show the digits from 0 to 9.) This activity is broadened in each of the three main fraction lessons in this section. Although it is not necessary to use them all, this introductory activity provides the basis for the others.

Note: It is possible to do this activity without a 10-sided die. Choose digits in another random way. (Directions for students are in italics.)

Here are some challenges that are appropriate for this point in the lesson.

1. Throw the 10-sided die 5 times, recording the numbers that result.

   Challenge: Use two of the numbers to make a fraction with the greatest possible value.

   Repeat the procedure a few times so that most students recognize the strategy.

   Discuss: Explain your strategy. How could a calculator be used to resolve disputes?

2. Throw the 10-sided die 4 times, recording the numbers that result.

   Challenge: Use each number only once and make

   - *the two fractions whose values are closest to 0*
   - *the two fractions whose values are closest to $\frac{1}{2}$*
   - *the two fractions whose values are closest to 1*
   - *the two fractions with the greatest values*

   Repeat the procedure so that students are confronted with various combinations. For example, special considerations occur when the number 0 appears. Zero cannot be placed in the denominator. They will have to use the 0 as one numerator and choose its denominator so that the other fraction meets the challenge optimally. For example, if the digits are 0, 9, 6, and 2, then the two fractions whose values are

   - closest to 0 are $\frac{0}{6}$ and $\frac{2}{9}$
   - closest to $\frac{1}{2}$ are $\frac{0}{9}$ and $\frac{2}{6}$ or $\frac{0}{2}$ and $\frac{6}{9}$
   - closest to 1 are $\frac{0}{2}$ and $\frac{6}{9}$
   - greatest are $\frac{0}{6}$ and $\frac{9}{2}$

   If two of the numbers are 0, the students should see that the numerators of both fractions must be 0 and that the placement of the other two numbers is arbitrary for all of the cases.

   Discuss: Explain the strategy you used in each case.

PAGES 156–157

Equivalent Fractions

Handout 5:
Rulers

TG page 114

Students need to "see" that there are many fractional names for the same number. This is the idea behind equivalent fractions. The close-up views of a ruler provide a concrete representation of this important fact. I used the ruler, a useful application of fractions, rather than pie drawings for this purpose. Numeracy involves proficiency in using a ruler as well as an understanding of fractions. From my classroom experience, it was apparent that many students could not measure with feet and inches. From the results of the feasibility study for the Adult Literacy and Lifeskills Survey, we are finding that this weakness is more widespread in the population than I had imagined.

At a recent conference, I saw a manipulative that demonstrates the differe names for the positions on a ruler more effectively than is possible with a static page in a book. It is called "The Master Ruler" and is available fro Master Innovations, Inc., P.O. Box 906, Alpha, NJ 08865-0906. Transp layers, each with successively smaller fractions of an inch, are bound t so that they can be discussed separately as well as in combination as t appear on an actual ruler.

Judy Storer and Pam Meader from Maine suggested another introdu the ruler page. They give students strips of paper to fold, first in ha fourths, and so on. After each fold, the students are asked to label the folds on the strip.

When your students are ready for page 156, each of them should have (1) an actual ruler to use as a reference and (2) a personal copy of a ruler that has been blown up to a size large enough to write on (Handout 5, TG page 114). You should also have a transparency of the blown-up rulers. Proceed by labeling the inches, then the half inches, and so forth (as the student book shows), allowing the ruler to function as a number line for each of the denominations. Students should write on their copies, noting the equivalencies as they occur.

It is important that students have a concrete representation of equal fractions to picture in their minds before they are taught the "Fundamental Principle of Equal Fractions" on page 157. This is an introduction to the topic of "reducing" fractions and "building" fractions that will be expanded in later lessons.

EXTENSION ACTIVITY

Measuring with Fractions   (small groups)

Take some time to teach your students how to use their rulers to measure actual objects. Expect them to name the ruler marking that each object comes to. You could begin this exercise by using a transparent ruler on the overhead projector to measure some strips of paper. Then ask each group to measure some common distances, like the space between the lines on their paper, the length and width of their books, the thickness of their desks, and so on.

GE 158

Fractions and Measurements

Writing fractional parts of different measures offers an everyday application of simplifying a fraction to lowest terms. The reverse of this procedure, for example, finding how many ounces there are in $\frac{1}{4}$ of a pound will be discussed in **Lesson 17**.

Fractions and Simple Probability

Here, students are asked to think of fractions as a way to write probabilities. They construct the fraction and simplify it if possible. You can extend **Problem 16** by asking students to put the 5 events described in order of the likelihood of their happening. In this way, the ideas of probability can inform their growing sense of the relative size of fractions.

nnect the ideas of probability of other randomly occurring events (having inning ticket in the lottery, picking a name of someone you know when domly select a name from the phone book, choosing the short straw in n process, and so on) by asking students to decide whether the oilities are close to 0, $\frac{1}{2}$, or 1.

PAGE 159

Calculator Exploration

The students are taught how to use the ⬛ a ᵇ/꜀ key to find the equivalents that were discussed in this lesson. If your students need more practice, go back to **Problems 5**, **10**, and **13**. You should emphasize, however, that the questions in these problems represent common, less difficult situations for which most of them will not need a calculator.

PAGES 160–161

Check Your Understanding and GED Practice

Problem 1 in Check Your Understanding and **Problem 4** in GED Practice ask students to use some of the most common fractions to estimate the size of fractions that have more unusual numerators and denominators.
In the lesson, students used $\frac{1}{2}$ to estimate the size of fractions; now they are asked to extend it to other fractions as well. The reasoning is similar to what students did in **Lesson 7**, when they rounded to compatible numbers in order to estimate answers to division problems.

Adding and Subtracting Fractions

OBECTIVES

Students will be able to

- picture adding and subtracting common fractions on a ruler or a number line
- use the rules to add and subtract common fractions and mixed numbers
- estimate answers to addition and subtraction problems that involve fractions other than the most common ones
- decide whether or not an estimate is sufficient for an everyday problem
- use the $a\,b/c$ key on the calculator to find precise answers to complex addition and subtraction problems with fractions

Background

Handout 6:
Fraction Table

TG page 115

Nearly everyone's experience is testimony to the fact that people quickly forget the rules of operating with fractions. For this reason, those rules are emphasized only with problems that can be visualized. The mechanics of the procedures should be secondary to being able to picture the problems on a ruler and estimating. So that students can readily picture the problems, each should have a copy of the Fraction Table (TG page 115) to use and write on as he or she wishes.

Lesson Recommendations

PAGES 162–164

Mental Math

The purpose of these mental math exercises is to review comparing fractions. This is a critical skill for students to have as they begin estimating with fractions.

Picturing Fractions

The fraction table extends the work students did with the ruler in **Lesson 15** to include thirds, sixths, fifths, and tenths. Insist that students use the table to visually find the answers to **Problems 1, 2,** and **3** before they use the manipulative procedures in **Problems 4** and **5**.

PAGES 164–166

Adding Fractions

Problem 7 uses only fractions that are on a ruler. Use a transparent copy of the ruler that is pictured and ask students to actually line up lengths of paper along this expanded scale to see where the sum falls for parts **A–F**. Since the sixteenths are marked but not labeled on this ruler, parts **G–J** will require some reasoning.

Problem 8 uses only the most common fractions when applying the rule for addition. Students should be getting comfortable with renaming and simplifying these by now. For the fractions (such as thirds, fifths, and tenths) that are not represented on a ruler, have students refer to the Fraction Table from page 162.

Problem 8❶ offers an opportunity to demonstrate the need for a common denominator when adding. Use a transparency of the Fraction Table (Handout 6, TG page 115) to show a strip of length $\frac{1}{2}$ being added to $\frac{1}{5}$.

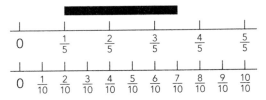

Where does the end of the strip fall? It falls between two of the one-fifth marks. To find a fraction that corresponds to this (a tic mark at exactly that point), students need to look down on the next number line marked in tenths to see the $\frac{7}{10}$ mark. Show the addition again using the tenths number line from the start to reinforce the manipulations that were done to find the answer.

PAGES 166–167

Subtracting Fractions

Begin again with picturing the problems in **Problem 11** on a ruler. Then, in **Problem 12**, use the rule, $\frac{a}{c} - \frac{b}{c} = \frac{a-b}{c}$ ($c \neq 0$), that states that a common denominator is also necessary for subtraction. By comparing the rules to the pictures, students can see that finding the common denominator merely assures that all the spaces on the number line are of the same size.

It is a common requirement to find what is left after a fractional part is taken away from a whole. We use denominators that are less common for these problems (**Problem 13**) because they often occur when dealing with probabilities.

Complementary Probabilities

Introduce this small section by reminding students that the probability of an event that is certain to happen is 1. Use a number cube and ask students for the probability of rolling a number less than 7. Since all the possible outcomes are favorable (they all satisfy the requirement), the event is *certain* to happen whenever a number cube is rolled. The same idea applies when you combine two possible outcomes that encompass all the possibilities; for example, rolling a 5 and rolling a number that is not 5. One or the other of these two outcomes has to happen, so the sum of their probabilities has to equal 1; we say they are complementary. Once this is clear, students can follow the equivalent equation strategy to see that $P(\text{not } 5) = 1 - P(5)$.

PAGES 168–169

Adding and Subtracting Mixed Numbers

Making mixed number problems easy to solve requires that students see that a plus (+) sign is understood to be between the whole number and fractional parts of a mixed number. Then they can apply the dependable principles they learned earlier about order and grouping when adding.

In the third example, when adding mixed numbers students encounter the one time that a fraction whose value is greater than 1 is an improper notation for an answer—$8\frac{9}{8}$ is not in simplest form. When a fraction is part of a mixed number, its value should be less than 1.

The procedure for borrowing in subtraction is not stressed here so that the students will focus on visualizing the fractions. In most cases with common fractions, students can picture their way through the problem (**Problem 15G**).

You can also introduce students to some common sense ways to think of borrowing. Start with an example like **Problem 15H**, $9 - 2\frac{1}{8}$. Write it as $9 - (2 + \frac{1}{8})$ which is equivalent to $9 - 2 - \frac{1}{8}$. Both the 2 and the $\frac{1}{8}$ must be subtracted from 9. Subtract 2 from 9 first, leaving 7. Then subtract $\frac{1}{8}$ from 7, leaving $6\frac{7}{8}$.

Another way to think of "borrowing" is to *add* the same number to both fractions. For example, try $5\frac{1}{8} - 2\frac{1}{4}$. Renaming leaves $5\frac{1}{8} - 2\frac{2}{8}$. *Choose* to add $\frac{6}{8}$ to both numbers. This makes the second number a whole number. The result, $5\frac{7}{8} - 3 = 2\frac{7}{8}$, is an easy problem to solve.

This is a "compensation" technique often used by mental math whizzes. It also works with whole numbers. This technique is shown in "Another Way to Subtract: Subtracting Without Borrowing," Appendix page 298.

PAGE 169

Adding and Subtracting Measurements

This section may be helpful in convincing students that the rule that says you must add and subtract "likes" to "likes" makes sense. It clearly applies to measurements (you wouldn't add 3 ft to 5 in. and get 8 ft-in.) and is consistently applied to fractions (can't add $\frac{2}{3}$ and $\frac{3}{4}$ to get $\frac{5}{7}$) and algebraic terms (can't add $4x$ and $7y$ to get $11xy$). The practical examples found in measurements reinforce the ideas of the previous sections.

PAGE 170

Calculator Exploration

Students and teachers alike will agree that using a calculator to find precise answers to problems like the ones listed is a wonderful technological advancement. At the same time, we recognize that it does not release us completely from learning the procedures. As stated earlier, learning the procedures with the commonly occurring fractions increases number and operation sense and provides the basis for estimating answers when the fractions are less common. You can predict that the non-calculator section of the GED test is *not* likely to include the requirement to perform the standard operations with uncommon fractions. At the same time, you should emphasize that throughout the test, the questions that involve fractions *will* likely depend on understanding the fundamental concepts.

PAGES 170–172

Estimating When Adding and Subtracting Fractions

This section is where students apply the concepts from **Lesson 15**. Not only will students be able to find an estimate that is "close to" the exact answer, but in many cases, they will also be able to tell whether the exact answer will be higher or lower than their estimate.

Again, students should be able to use their common sense along with their developing problem-solving skills. They should be able to come up with answers that are acceptable for most situations in everyday life as well as discriminating enough to indicate the right answer choices on the GED Test.

Underlying the techniques outlined in the student book is the principle that, for every difficult problem, there is an easy one nearby to compare it to. The answer needed should be "close to" (and close enough to) the answer of the easy problem. Encourage your students to be inventive in finding these comparisons. Remind them that the examples in the answer key represent only one possible means of solution.

EXTENSION ACTIVITY

Fractions from Random Numbers   (in pairs)

Revisit the activity with the 10-sided die from the previous lesson. At this point, the following challenge is appropriate:

Throw the 10-sided die 6 times, recording the numbers that result.

Challenge: Use any four of the numbers (can be different numbers for each case) to make two fractions that

- add to a number that is closest to 0
- subtract leaving a number that is closest to 0
- add to a number that is closest to $\frac{1}{2}$
- add to a number that is closest to 1
- add to the greatest total
- subtract leaving the greatest number

Discuss: Explain your strategy for each case.

PAGE 172

Adding and Subtracting Fractions in Real Situations

By now, your students are aware of how close to the exact answer they can get by estimating. This should encourage them to estimate more in their everyday lives. The examples and problems point out the sufficiency of an estimate in some common situations that involve fractions. Ask your students to recall times in their lives when estimating with fractions would have been adequate. Discuss how this awareness can give a person more control over the numbers in his or her life.

PAGE 173

Using Data

The vocation of carpentry is one of the most likely to require people to be skilled at manipulating exactly with fractions. Carry on your discussion of situations that require or don't require precise computations with fractions by asking for student opinions about the situations described in this activity. If you have students in your class with experience in carpentry, they may be able to reveal their techniques for covering up an inexact fit between components. For example, molding between a wall and a built-in cabinet covers up the fact that one or the other may not be exactly plumb.

Multiplying and Dividing Fractions

OBJECTIVES

Students will

- recognize which operation to apply to fractional situations (where *of* means to multiply)
- multiply and divide fractions, canceling when possible
- multiply fractions to find the probability of independent and dependent events
- estimate when finding fractional parts of a number by rounding to a compatible number

Background

Confusion arises with multiplication and division of fractions mainly because of the vocabulary commonly used to discuss the situations. To add to the confusion, students often believe that when they multiply, the answer must be greater than the original number. Although they have already seen multiplication by a number less than 1 (**Lesson 9,** page 94), they will need to be reminded that when multiplying by a number less than 1, they should expect a smaller answer (when the numbers involved are positive).

Lesson Recommendations

PAGES 176–177

Mental Math

The purpose of these mental math exercises is to reinforce students' understanding of the relative size of fractions.

Finding a Fraction of a Fraction

The sketches *show* students that when they multiply by a fraction less than 1, they should expect an answer that is less than the original number. The visual is reinforced when the word *of* is stressed (for example, $\frac{1}{4}$ *of* $\frac{3}{8}$ is less than $\frac{3}{8}$). Reemphasize this point with each exercise in **Problem 1**.

PAGES 177–178

Finding a Fraction of a Whole Number and Canceling

Finding fractional parts of numbers is the most common everyday use for fractions. For example, students already know the fractional parts of an hour. In addition, it is closely related to finding a percent of a number, the topic of later lessons. Expect your students to master these skills.

If your students can cancel, they can make these problems even easier. However, be sure to point out that failing to notice the opportunity to cancel and multiplying the original numbers does not make the answer wrong. They will just have to simplify the answer.

You should caution that canceling is an option *only* when *multiplying* with fractions. Students often go overboard and cancel indiscriminately; they use it incorrectly when adding fractions or when solving proportions. Recommend that students look for the multiplication sign before they think about canceling.

Using Data

The graphs summarize some of the recent advice as to asset allocation at different stages in one's life. The underlying principle is that if you won't need your money in the immediate future, you can better afford to invest where the risks (and rewards) are greater. Since many of the fractions have denominators of 10 and the amounts are multiples of powers of 10, canceling offers an opportunity to review the shortcut of moving the decimal point when you divide by 10.

PAGE 179

Probability: Independent and Dependent Events

The probability principle involved with successive *independent* events can be pictured using tree diagrams.

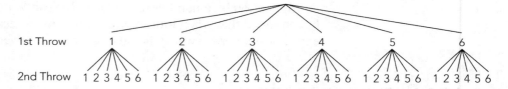

Only one of the 36 possible outcomes consists of 2 sixes.

Since this is a "for each" situation—that is, for each possibility on the first throw, there are 6 possibilities on the second—your students should not be surprised that multiplication is the operation to use here.

When the result of the first event affects the possible outcomes of the second, the two events are said to be *dependent*. Again, the two probabilities are multiplied to find the probability of both happening.

PAGE 180

Multiplying Mixed Numbers

Students tend to want to repeat the strategy from adding mixed numbers and merely multiply the whole numbers and then multiply the fractions. The fact that the expansion of the sample problem $2\frac{1}{2} \times 1\frac{3}{4}$ is $(2 + \frac{1}{2}) \times (1 + \frac{3}{4})$, uses *both* addition and multiplication signs, means that one cannot just group the whole numbers and fractions. Instead, the addition in the parentheses must be done before the multiplication.

With small numbers, the addition step is accomplished by making the mixed number a single fraction. The multiplication step follows, then the answer is changed back to a mixed number. However, this method will result in tedious computations when the numbers get large, for example, in a problem like $32\frac{2}{9} \times 53\frac{11}{12}$. For this reason, I recommend using a calculator or estimating for problems like these if and when they ever occur in a realistic situation.

The distributive property underlies the method suggested for multiplying a mixed number times a whole number. Applications for this procedure are common, especially when units of measure are involved, as in **Problem 10**.

PAGE 181

Estimating Fractional Parts

Canceling is very important when estimation and mental math are stressed, as they are in this book. Canceling can make the difference between students needing paper and pencil and being able to find the answer in their heads.

To be able to cancel for the problems on this page, the prices need to be rounded to a number that is compatible to the denominator of the fraction—that is, they must be easily divisible by the denominator. Rounding to the nearest 10 or 100 may not result in a problem that lends itself to estimating, so caution your students to focus first on the denominator and then round the prices.

Extend the two problems by asking students to compare each estimated answer with the precise calculator answer. Students should be gaining confidence with estimation in consumer applications.

PAGE 182

Dividing Fractions

The example, 6 divided by $\frac{1}{4}$, allows students to see the reasoning behind the rule for division by a fraction. Beyond that, it also leads to an interpretation of a division situation that is critical for understanding what answer to expect. "How many quarter-inches are there in 1? So, how many are there in 6?"

The same question "How many __'s are there in ___?" was introduced as an interpretation of a division situation in **Lesson 7**. The question is also used to make sense of the answers in **Problem 13**. You could use the blown-up ruler (TG page 114) to offer visual explanations for some of the problems and their answers.

Fractions from Random Numbers   (in pairs)

Revisit the activity with the 10-sided die from the previous lessons. The point of the following challenge is to decide whether the greatest or least possible fraction will give the desired result. The ideas were first introduced in **Lesson 9**.

Throw the 10-sided die 5 times, recording the numbers that result.

Challenge: Choose 2 numbers (can be different in each case) to make a fraction $\left(\frac{a}{b}\right)$ *that*

- *gives the expression* $(10 \times \frac{a}{b})$ *the greatest possible value*
- *gives the expression* $(10 \times \frac{a}{b})$ *the least possible value*
- *gives the expression* $(10 \div \frac{a}{b})$ *the greatest possible value*
- *gives the expression* $(10 \div \frac{a}{b})$ *the least possible value*

Discuss: Explain the reasoning that you used to choose the numbers in each case.

PAGE 183

Calculator Exploration

Since there are no new calculator techniques to learn here, use this opportunity to make students aware of the components of problem solving that they must be able to accomplish in addition to what the calculator does. As before, they need to have the number sense to know whether or not the answer displayed on the calculator is reasonable. For this lesson particularly, students must be able to decide *when* to multiply and divide. They will continue to multiply when they combine equal groups (part **E**) and divide to find how many equal groups are present (part **F**). In addition, this lesson introduces multiplication as the operation to use when they are asked to find a fractional part of something (parts **G**, **H**, **I**). If students are not sure of the operation, they can ask themselves whether the question "How many _____s are there in _____?" correctly interprets the situation. If the question correctly interprets the situation, as in part **F**, division is the operation to use. If it does not, as in part **I**, do not divide.

PAGE 184

Check Your Understanding

At first glance, the equations in **Problem 5** may look intimidating. A closer look shows that although they contain fractions, the equations require only one step to solve. The equations provide a review and an extension of earlier algebraic methods—students "undo" the operation shown so that the variable is isolated on its side of the equation.

OBJECTIVES

By reviewing the relationship between fractions and decimals, students will

- recognize the decimal equivalents of common fractions and find the equivalents of the eighths and sixths
- find the answer to problems using either decimals or fractions
- see the connections between the ways the operations are completed with fractions and decimals
- explore the relationship between original price, discount, and sale price, and solve problems involving these quantities
- recognize the options available when solving multistep problems involving fractions

Background

We cannot expect our students to synthesize the parts of a course of study into an organized whole without some help. The purpose of this lesson is to aid students in comparing the new information from this chapter on fractions with what they did in prior lessons with decimals. In some cases, their knowledge of fractions will help them understand why the decimal methods worked, and in other cases, the opposite will be true. When students understand the comparisons, they will have more options for solving problems. They will become more flexible problem solvers. So, while this lesson could be considered a review, it also has an important purpose of its own.

Lesson Recommendations

PAGES 186–187

Mental Math

These exercises provide an opportunity for students to discover patterns and make connections between numbers.

Decimals and Fractions

Handout 6:
Fraction Table

TG page 115

Give each student a paper copy of the Fraction Table (TG page 115). Use it to record the decimal equivalents that are called for in **Problem 1**. The completed table will be used as a reference on the next page, **Using Data**, part **C**. Expect that your students should be able to write the equivalents for most of the lines without referring to their calculators. For the more unfamiliar lines (eighths and sixths), students can use the structure of the table as a guide and discover how to determine these decimal equivalents from the ones that they have memorized.

Starting with the first number line, label each tic mark with its decimal equivalent. The first difficulty may occur when they get to the line marked in eighths. On this line, students should begin by labeling the equivalents that are identical to the previous line.

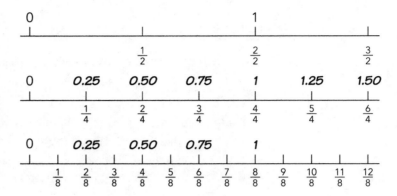

When students notice from the structure of the table that $\frac{1}{8}$ is half of $\frac{1}{4}$, they reason that to find the decimal equivalent of $\frac{1}{8}$, they need to find half of 0.25. Similarly, to find the equivalent of $\frac{3}{8}$, they need to find the number halfway between 0.25 and 0.50, and so on.

Encourage students to use the same strategy to find the sixths. They can write these as repeating decimals or you could show them how to use fractions for the remainders after two decimal places ($0.16\frac{2}{3}$, $0.33\frac{1}{3}$, $0.66\frac{2}{3}$, $0.83\frac{1}{3}$).

Later, students can check their results by entering the fraction into the calculator as a division problem: $\frac{3}{8} = 0.375$ or $0.37\frac{1}{2}$, $\frac{5}{6} = 0.833...$ or $0.83\frac{1}{3}$, and so on.

Problem 2 explains that finding the average of two numbers (adding them and dividing by 2) is one way to find the number that is halfway between them.

Using Data

If you have the technology available, this activity is a perfect opportunity for you to introduce the use of a computer spreadsheet. Entering the formulas for columns 2 and 5 and ordering the results for columns 3 and 6 are meaningful learning experiences and also show the power of the software.

The last column requires students to use one of the common fractions from the table they completed in **Problem 1** to estimate the decimal values found in column 5. Finding the fraction whose decimal equivalent is closest to the each value in column 5 is not difficult. Sports fans will recognize that announcers for the games often use the common fraction format to report on a quarterback's effectiveness.

Solving Problems with Decimals and Fractions

Students who know the decimal equivalents of fractions will be able to estimate answers for a large variety of real-life problems. On this page, students are taught to be more flexible in their problem-solving strategies when finding the exact answers. Students will find that when they choose fractions, they are able to find the answers without their calculators and when they choose decimals, they would prefer to use the calculator.

Discuss the pros and cons of each strategy. Using fractions is often faster, especially when you add in the time necessary to locate a calculator. Those who are less confident of their computation skills will prefer to depend on the calculator so they can be sure of their answers.

PAGES 189–190

Fraction and Decimal Operations

Comparing the methods for addition, subtraction, multiplication, and division of fractions with the methods previously used for decimals will validate both sets of procedures. This helps students understand why they did what they did and also helps them remember what to do when. If they forget, there's a good chance they can figure out the procedure from their understanding of the other form.

The connections between most of the operations are explained for the student. However, **Problem 4** challenges students to make the connection between the rule for multiplying decimals and what they did for fractions.

Placing the decimal point in the answer of multiplication and division problems can also be done using estimation. For practice, ask students to estimate in order to choose the correct answer in the following problems:

$562.4 \times 2.11 =$	**Ⓐ** 118.6664	**Ⓑ** 1,186.664	**Ⓒ** 11,866.64
$103 \times 0.35 =$	**Ⓐ** 3,605	**Ⓑ** 360.5	**Ⓑ** 36.05
$54.35 \div 8.75 =$	**Ⓐ** 6.2114285	**Ⓑ** 62.114285	**Ⓑ** 6,211.4285

PAGES 191–193

Multistep Problems

Discount and sale price are discussed a number of times in the student book, and they will be revisited during the percent section.

Some of your students will recognize that the two methods for solving these problems are really just examples of the distributive property. The example on page 191 shows students that they can either multiply first $[240(1 - \frac{1}{4}) = 240 - (\frac{1}{4} \times 240)]$ or subtract first $[240(1 - \frac{1}{4}) = 240(\frac{3}{4})]$ to solve the problem.

A less common application (found in **Problem 9**) is that of finding the original price when the sale price and the fraction of discount are known. The common error here is to use the sale price as the base for the discount. The question "$\frac{3}{4}$ of *what*?" will provide the focus that is needed here as well as in future lessons with percent.

Other Multistep Problems

The two-step problems in this section combine fractions and decimals in realistic situations that are actually likely to contain both formats.

Test-Taking Tips

OBJECTIVES

Students will

- review the methods and concepts of this unit
- increase their test-taking skill with multistep problems
- evaluate their progress

Lesson Recommendations

PAGE 196

Multistep Problems

A good multiple-choice test item offers incorrect answer alternatives that tempt the examinee to choose them. This is not meant as a trick, but as a technique to make the assessment a sound one.

When constructing items that involve many steps, item writers know that examinees often lose track of what the question asks and stop solving before they get to the final step. For this reason, item writers often use the interim answers as incorrect answer alternatives.

The example cautions students about this practice and shows that the partial (or interim) answers are listed among the choices given. Students can avoid making this common error if they use the strategy of writing the problem as a single expression before they start any calculations.

To simulate the actual time given for the GED Test, allow students about 40 minutes to complete all of the questions. The test in this lesson features two sections, the first where calculators are allowed and the second where they are not. The actual test is structured in this way and follows strict administration policies. At the start, examinees are given the calculator and the calculator section of the test and are allowed half the total test time to complete it. When that time is up or when they finish, whichever comes first, examinees will turn in their calculators and be given the second part of the test. Note that this means that they have the opportunity to go back to the first part of the test during the second half, but they will not be allowed the use of a calculator.

Although it has been hinted at in earlier Test-Taking Tips lessons, it is important for you to make sure that students see that many items in the calculator section do not lend themselves to using one. They are thought of as being calculator-neutral and often would be classified cognitively as being "conceptual." Emphasizing this fact will prompt students to focus on the other components of problem solving in addition to the computation component. Remind students that there is more to this math test than computation procedures.

Also note that this set of items is unusually high in the percentage of items that involve fractions. You have probably noticed that in the official published practice tests, only a small percentage of the items actually require knowledge of fraction operations.

Discuss and extend the items in this lesson by encouraging students to reveal their unique strategies for choosing answers and by inventing other questions that could have been asked about the situations described in the items.

PAGES 197–201

Check Your Skills

The distributive property is involved in both **Problems 10** and **11**. When writing the mathematical expression for **Problem 10**, students would likely begin with either $(4\frac{1}{2} + \frac{1}{2} + 3)(\$8.50)$ or $4\frac{1}{2}(\$8.50) + 1\frac{1}{2}(\$8.50) + 3(\$8.50)$, neither of which is listed as an alternative. If your students picked either alternative (1) or (5), which are made to resemble these two expressions, they need to be reminded of paying attention to the details. In both cases, multiplication signs are used instead of addition signs.

In **Problem 11**, finding the average of 3 measurements is made more complex because the measurements have been reported in different formats. Although the answer key shows the problem being done with fractions, students have also learned to add the measurements themselves (page 169).

$$\frac{3 \text{ ft } 6 \text{ in.} + 3 \text{ ft } 4 \text{ in.} + 2 \text{ ft } 8 \text{ in.}}{3} = \frac{8 \text{ ft } 18 \text{ in.}}{3} \text{ or } \frac{9 \text{ ft } 6 \text{ in.}}{3} = 3 \text{ ft } 2 \text{ in.}$$

Problems 15 and **16** are grouped under the information that defines an isosceles triangle. Students cannot expect that definitions and resulting assumptions will always be provided on the test, so they should be prepared to answer these two questions even without the information. For **Problem 15** the fact that angles X and Z are equal results in the equation (for the sum of the angles in a triangle) $180 = 30 + 2x$, which is solved by subtracting 30 from both sides and then dividing both sides by 2.

Problem 16 is an example that is a bit artificial because of the constraints caused by the coordinate-plane-grid answer format. If the answer could have been a point anywhere on the plane, rather than only a point whose x- and y-coordinates were integers, there would have been many other possible answers. (You could show other possible answers by drawing a line from point A to point B, and then drawing a perpendicular line though the estimated midpoint of line AB. Any point on the perpendicular line is a possible third vertex (C) of an isosceles triangle, where AC and BC are the equal sides.)

You can have an interesting discussion about probabilities by extending **Problem 17** with some additional questions. "If Jasmine did not get the short straw, what is the probability that the next one to choose will get it?" (1 out of 4) This question is worded so that the two events are considered separately and not in combination. If you were to consider the overall probability that the second person to draw would get the short straw, you would have to multiply the probability that the first one wouldn't get it by the probability that the second one would. ($\frac{4}{5} \times \frac{1}{4} = \frac{1}{5}$, the same probability that the first one had of getting the short straw.) When you carry this reasoning out to all 5 of the participants, you will see that each one does have an equal chance of getting the short straw, in theory as well as intuitively.

Problems 21 and **22** can be answered by estimating with the graph or by solving the equation that is given. Point out to students that even without the equation, they could have been sure of choosing the correct estimate. None of the other alternatives were within the bounds of the two lines on the graph that enclosed the correct one.

If your class size permits, arrange to discuss student errors with each one individually. Use this evaluation to diagnose common difficulties and tailor your instruction in the last section to compensate for them.

EXTENSION ACTIVITY

"I Have, Who Has?" Review

If you have more class time, play a round of "I Have, Who Has?" using the new concepts. (Refer to the explanation given in **Lesson 14** on TG page 65.) For example, this set of 10 index cards would be appropriate:

I have 12.	Who has $\frac{1}{3}$ of this?
I have 4.	Who has this squared?
I have 16.	Who has $\frac{1}{2}$ of this?
I have 8.	Who has 3 times this?
I have 24.	Who has 6 more?
I have 30.	Who has $\frac{1}{10}$ of this?
I have 3.	Who has $\frac{1}{3}$ of this?
I have 1.	Who has $\frac{1}{4}$ of this?
I have 0.25.	Who has this times 16?
I have 4.	Who has the number of thirds in this?

You may wish to write the problems on the board as they occur; sometimes it is difficult to picture canceling without the written problem.

Comparisons: Fractions as Ratios

OBJECTIVES

Students will

- write ratios and rates describing comparisons
- use unit rates to compare different rates
- appreciate the wide spectrum of situations for which ratios are applicable and recognize when they are not applicable
- express ratios in simplest form
- recognize relationships present in a proportion
- use the Law of Proportionality to determine whether or not two fractions are equivalent

Background

Connecting Prior Knowledge with Ratio and Proportions

Your students already have a strong background as they begin this chapter on ratio and proportion. They learned the relationship between multiplication and division by exploring two "rate" relationships, $d = rt$ and $c = nr$. They know that the line in a fraction means "divided by." This section on ratio and proportion builds on these concepts and lays the groundwork for the study of percents and the application of slopes.

The reasoning and strategies involving proportional relationships are some of the most practical math skills for solving problems that occur in our daily lives. These situations are most often the ones that confront people and demand that they use the math they learned in school. Because the topic is so widely applicable and because it cannot be understood adequately by merely learning one procedure, I have included a discussion of alternate lines of reasoning and methods of solution in this last section. Moreover, you may have recognized how the structure of the entire student book has fostered a mind-set that ensures that students will be ready to analyze the relationships, choose efficient strategies, and use estimation to judge reasonableness when solving the problems in this section on ratio, proportion, and percent. Students' number sense, problem-solving attitudes, and beliefs in their own competence are enmeshed in the approach to these final important topics.

This first lesson serves as an introduction to ratio and proportion. It includes a variety of rate applications, the picturing of a rate as the slope of a line on a graph, the relationships between numbers in a proportion, and the fundamental Law of Proportionality. All these topics will be revisited in later lessons, with the law of proportionality serving as the foundation for one method of solving proportions, including percents.

Lesson Recommendations

PAGES 202–203

Mental Math

The purpose of these exercises is to review what students know about simplifying and building fractions to become equivalent ones.

Using Ratios (or Fractions) to Compare

Introduce your students to the three ways to write a ratio. Of course, the most mathematical way (fraction form) is the one we will pursue. Point out to students that there are different ways to represent the same relationship. In the example, the $\frac{\text{married}}{\text{single}}$ student ratio is $\frac{11}{5}$ while the $\frac{\text{single}}{\text{married}}$ student ratio is $\frac{5}{11}$. Both are valid ratios for the relationship. To determine which ratio to use in **Problem 1**, students must look for the order of the words in the problem. If they use the same order as the words, they will be correct. When they set up proportions in later problems, they will have the freedom to choose the order.

PAGES 203–205

Rates

When quantities of unlike units of measure are being compared in a ratio, it is called a *rate*. To make sense, the units of measure must be included in the final answer.

Calculator Exploration

Comparing by using unit rates is based on the idea of standardizing the two different rates—that is, finding what the rates would be if expressed in terms of 1 unit (price for 1 ounce, salary for 1 month, dollars for 1 peso, and so on). Unit rates have become more available to consumers as more supermarkets post the unit-price labels on the shelves below items. Without a calculator the precise computation would be tedious, but we will estimate unit rates in the next lesson.

EXTENSION ACTIVITY

Unit Rates for Familiar Items   (Individual or small groups)

Make the unit price idea more personal by asking students to report the prices of various package sizes of an item that they regularly use. They should find specific examples on their next shopping trip or you could arrange to accompany a group of them to a nearby supermarket after class.

Using Data

Nutrition labels on foods provide the stimulus for this study of rates. Students analyze the specific data given on the labels of various snack foods and use the input to make a generalization about an interesting rate, the number of calories in a gram of fat in foods. Differences in the methods of analysis and subsequent rounding mean that the reported rates will vary slightly, but they are close enough to indicate a trend.

In small print on the bottom of some labels, you will find a statement that there are 9 calories in 1 gram of fat, even though the data in the label does not conform exactly to this fact. It would be interesting to learn more about the procedures that cause food companies to continue with this apparent discrepancy.

The "line of best fit" represents the result of a statistical procedure, least squares regression, which is widely used to make generalizations and predictions from individual data points. It is beyond the scope of this course, but you should know that there is a great deal of mathematics that underlies the simple presentation given in the student book.

PAGES 206–207

Slopes: Picturing Rates on a Graph

The graph of one racer's performance during a triathlon provides a visual representation of the varying rates for the different phases. In addition, it is an example of a graph that tells a story of an event happening over time. Discuss the horizontal line segments and ask how the graph would picture a hypothetical racer retracing his path to go back and correct the fact that he swam on the wrong side of a buoy. (Because time is passing, the line would not retrace the line that is already drawn, but would slope downward during his swim back to the buoy.)

The fact that a steeper slope illustrates a faster rate is fundamental to interpreting graphs. Of course, this is true only when the lines are on the same graph or when the scales of the two axes of different graphs are proportional.

Slopes of lines will be discussed again later when the slope formula $\left(\frac{y^2 - y^1}{x^2 - x^1} \right)$ is introduced. This introduction allows an exploration of the basic idea of the ratio without involving the coordinate plane or its complex formula.

PAGES 207–209

Expressing Ratios in Simplest Form

Students are reminded of the mechanics of simplifying fractions as they are made aware of the convention that all ratios should be expressed in simplest form. This reminder is well placed before the formal ideas of proportions are introduced; students should recognize that their old skills are still relevant.

Equal Ratios Are Proportions

The student book points out three relationships that exist between the four numbers in a proportion. They are noted so that students will have options when they solve problems. The first relationship is merely a review of how to build equal fractions by multiplying the numerator and denominator by the same non-zero number. Instruct students to look across the two equal fractions to find the relationship that must be the same for numerators as well as denominators in a proportion.

The second relationship exists between the top and bottom of a single fraction. That relationship is the same in the other fraction of the proportion. You can call it the "within" relationship because it exists *within* the fraction. This is the relationship one used in solving analogies in literal applications. Depending on how one sets up a proportion, it could be described using the idea of a "factor of change." (Notice in **Problem 9B** how 8 is doubled to get 16; the factor of change is 2.) The book often uses this relationship as a mental check to see whether or not the answer seems to be correct.

The third relationship is important enough to be a principle. The Law of Proportionality will be used to solve proportions as well as percent problems. It states that if two ratios are equal, their cross products are equal. In this lesson, it is introduced and used to determine whether or not two fractions (ratios) are equal.

PAGES 210-211

When to Use Ratios and Proportions in Problems

Not all comparisons can be expressed with a ratio. You can make this apparent to your students by making some observations about the room you are in. If there are 8 students and 12 student desks, you could compare the number of students to desks by using the ratio $\frac{8}{12}$. On the other hand, you could also compare the number of students to desks by saying that there are 4 fewer students than desks. This statement compares by subtraction and does not involve ratios.

EXTENSION ACTIVITY

Everyday Ratios and Rates (whole class)

Ask students to look in newspapers or magazines for examples of ratios being used to compare numbers. They will find countless examples of percentages, but ask them to look further for other simple ratios. Other simple ratios can be anything from "4 out of 5 doctors surveyed" to "gale-force winds of 80 mph."

Proportions

OBJECTIVES

Students will

- set up a proportion that reflects the relationship in a real situation
- find the missing number in a proportion
- use proportions to solve problems involving similar figures
- determine the better buy by comparing estimates of unit prices

Background

Practical Ratio and Proportion Techniques

This lesson continues to expand students' awareness of the practicality of ratio and proportion techniques. The method of cross multiplication is used to solve proportions. However, students (and the teacher) must remain flexible with respect to this technique. From the start of a problem, they must be aware that there are many correct ways to set up a proportion, even though the answer key shows only one possibility. After the proportion is set up, encourage students to notice different patterns that may help them to solve the problem in an easier way than the structured algorithm of cross multiplication.

Lesson Recommendations

PAGE 214–215

Mental Math

Your students now know another way to determine the equality of fractions. Encourage them to use more than one method on these problems.

Seeing Proportions in Situations

Problems 1ⓗ and **1ⓘ** alert students to the different questions that can be asked but also introduce the need to deduce a missing value. If 2 out of 5 people are men, the students must deduce that 3 out of 5 are women. If the ratio of men to women is 2 to 3, they must deduce that the total is 5.

PAGES 215–216

Finding a Missing Number in a Proportion

After a review of solving equations involving multiplication, this section introduces the algorithm of solving proportions by cross multiplication. While students are encouraged to use their calculator whenever they wish, you should always point out ways to do problems without a calculator. Method 2 on page 216 shows how canceling makes the numbers easy enough to work with mentally.

PAGE 217

Fractions and Mixed Numbers in Proportions

Some of your students (especially the ones with lingering "fraction fear") will want to change the fractions to decimals in these proportions. Of course, that is acceptable. However, those who use decimals may need to use a calculator, while those who use fractions can solve these problems mentally.

To guard against the "mindless mimicry mathematics" that has dominated math instruction and learning, students are encouraged to step back after writing the proportion and examine it for other possible ways to find the answer. If the relationships are not obvious to them immediately, instruct them to look for the possibility of simplifying the ratio. If no apparent pattern emerges, then students can resort to cross multiplying. It is the standard method that they can always use.

PAGES 218–219

Using Proportions to Solve Real Problems

The examples on page 218 show students that they can apply the method of proportions to problems that are similar to those they have solved previously. Setting up the proportion correctly and carrying out the cross multiplication ensures choosing correctly between multiplication and division. For some of your students, this method will give them a safe, structured way to solve rate conversion problems.

EXTENSION ACTIVITY

Converting Units with Unit Rates (Dimensional Analysis)
(whole class)

In **Problem 5**, students used the structure of a proportion to help them decide whether to divide or multiply the significant numbers when converting from one unit of measurement to another. The method is a good one to use when there is a single conversion required and only one conversion factor is involved. In scientific applications, a conversion is often repeated for many values and there are often numerous conversion factors to consider. In science classes, teachers prefer to use the technique of dimensional analysis, a method that can accommodate the complex rate conversions that are required, for example, converting feet per second to miles per hour.

Introduce the technique by looking at the "Walking Speed Conversion Chart" on page 287 in the Appendix. The goal will be to determine mathematically how each column was determined from the other. Do you multiply or divide, and by what number?

Focus first on the easier conversion, from minutes per mile to miles per hour. Most students will recognize that the conversion fact that relates the two rates is that there are 60 minutes in each hour, which can be written as a ratio either as

$$\frac{60 \text{ min}}{1 \text{ hr}} \quad \text{or as} \quad \frac{1 \text{ hr}}{60 \text{ min}}$$

(Both fractions are equal to 1 since the numerator equals the denominator.)

Choose one line from the table (say, 15 min per mile) and set up the initial and desired ratios.

Initial Ratio × Conversion factor(s) = Desired ratio

Write this ——▶ $\dfrac{1\ mi}{15\ min}$ ratio with 'miles' on top.

$\dfrac{?\ mi}{1\ hr}$ ◀—— because this ratio has 'miles' on top.

Next, insert the conversion factor written so that the units you want to eliminate (in this case, minutes) will cancel.

Initial Ratio × Conversion factor(s) = Desired ratio

$$\dfrac{1\ mi}{15\ \cancel{min}} \quad \times \quad \dfrac{60\ \cancel{min}}{1\ hr} \quad = \quad \dfrac{?\ mi}{1\ hr}$$

Notice that the formatting that you have done with the measurement units leaves 60 in the numerator and 15 in the denominator. Their positions tell you to divide 60 by 15.

Initial Ratio × Conversion factor(s) = Desired ratio

$$\dfrac{1\ mi}{\underset{1}{\cancel{15}}\ \cancel{min}} \quad \times \quad \dfrac{\overset{4}{\cancel{60}}\ \cancel{min}}{1\ hr} \quad = \quad \dfrac{?\ mi}{1\ hr}$$

Set up the ratios for other lines in the chart to validate that you have found the mathematical rule behind the conversion between these two columns, that is, to divide 60 by the number of minutes per mile. Point out that dividing by the variable was to be expected since the values in one column increased while the other decreased.

Your students will probably not be impressed by the dimensional analysis method when it is used on such an easy conversion. To convince them of its value, go through the same procedure asking how the second column was determined from the first.

steps per minute ——▶ minutes per mile

Initial Ratio × Conversion factor(s) = Desired ratio

Write this ratio ——▶ $\dfrac{1\ min}{105\ steps}$ with 'minutes' on top.

$\dfrac{?\ min}{1\ mi}$ ◀—— because this ratio has 'minutes' on top.

For this conversion, two conversion factors are needed: the number of steps per mile and the number of feet in a mile. The following formats will allow the canceling of units.

Initial Ratio × Conversion factor(s) = Desired ratio

$$\dfrac{1\ min}{105\ \cancel{steps}} \quad \times \quad \dfrac{1\ \cancel{step}}{2.5\ \cancel{ft}} \times \dfrac{5280\ \cancel{ft}}{1\ mi} \quad = \quad \dfrac{?\ min}{1\ mi}$$

Again, the structure dictates which numbers to multiply and divide. Here, 5,280 is divided by both 105 and 2.5. The answer rounds to 20 minutes per mile.

Repeat the procedure for a few more lines of the chart. Notice again that the variable (steps per minute) is being divided into a constant so the numbers in the second column decrease while those in the first column increase.

PAGE 219

Using Data

This activity with data about the most popular movies over the years extends the ideas of proportional reasoning to a topic that may capture your students' imagination. Your students may not be movie buffs, but they are probably well aware of the recent hikes in movie ticket prices.

If your students did the previous activity, they will have a choice of methods to use in these problems. In these problems, students are asked to find what the prices of some consumer goods would have been if they assume that the price of all goods changed in the same proportion as movie tickets have over the years.

A. Method 1 (using proportions) *Gone with the Wind*

$$\frac{\$198.7 \text{ mill (in 1939)}}{\$1{,}187.7 \text{ mil (in 2002 dollars)}} = \frac{\$? \text{ (in 1939) for car}}{\$25{,}000 \text{ (in 2002)}}$$

A. Method 2 (using conversion factors) *Gone with the Wind*

$$\frac{\$25{,}000 \text{ (2002 dollars) for car}}{1} \times \frac{\$198.7 \text{ (1939 dollars)}}{\$1{,}187.7 \text{(2002 dollars)}} = \$? \text{ (1939 dollars)}$$

PAGES 220–221

Similar Triangles

Congruent figures have both the same shape and the same size. By itself, congruency does not define an interesting GED problem, but it can play an important role as a condition to consider when finding relationships between the components of geometrical figures.

When figures are similar, their angles are equal, but their sides are proportional. In the second example, the fact that the shadows are measured at the same time and that both the tree and the post are assumed to be perpendicular to the ground are what ensures that the angles in the two triangles are indeed equal.

PAGES 221–222

Using Similar Figures

The idea of similarity can be applied to any geometric figure; on page 222 it is applied in problems where scale drawings or maps are drawn to represent actual buildings or roads.

PAGE 223

Unit Rates Revisited

All of the examples for **Problem 13** came from one fact-finding trip to the supermarket. If your class is small and students seem interested in this topic, organize a shopping trip to compare prices. If this is not feasible, compare the food advertisements that appear from the different markets in your city.

Although we are focusing on estimation as a method to use with unit prices, we don't want to lose sight of the many different ways to compare prices. For example, students could set up the ratios differently, or they could compare the differences in number of ounces to differences in price. For **Problem 13**, encourage flexibility in the reasoning approaches that students use.

Some Tasty Comparisons (small groups)

You may have noted that some of the problems in the ratio and proportion lessons referred to the color of certain candies. You can use packages of candies, where many different colors of candies are present. It is presumed that the number of candies of each of the different colors is a random occurrence.

There are a wide variety of problems that you can create with bags of these candies. Invite students to do the following:

- Compare the contents of many packages. "What is the mean and median of the total number of candies in your packages?"

- Write ratios that compare the number of different colored candies. "What is the ratio of red candies to the total?" "Which color of candies is the least represented?" "What is the ratio of red candies to the candies of the least represented color?" "Is the ratio consistent between packages?"

- Compare packages of different sizes. "What is the total number of candies in each?" Compare the unit price of the candies in each size package. Use the ratios found in the small package to predict the number of a certain color of candies in the large package. "Do the color ratios remain consistent?"

- Keep a record of your findings and then use them as a resource in asking probability questions like, "What is the probability that the first candy that I pick out of this unopened bag is a red one?" or "What is the probability that the first two candies out of this bag are yellow?

If students save their results, they can use them again in the next lesson on percents.

Percent I

OBJECTIVES

Students will

- find missing numbers in easy percent relationships either mentally or with a few pencil strokes
- solve more complicated percent problems by using either proportions or equation solving
- write a percent equation that describes a problem situation
- recognize the role that the *base* of the percent plays

Background

Relating Percents with Decimals and Fractions

This first of two percent lessons starts by making the connection between percents and decimals. Percent means "hundredths" as well as "out of a hundred." The lesson then asks students to find missing numbers in percent relationships mentally. Only after they are comfortable with the idea of percent are the formal solution methods discussed.

Rather than present a rule for solving percent problems that applies only to percents, the methods for solution used in this lesson are adaptations of procedures that the students have already learned. Emphasize these connections so that the students see mathematics as a unified subject rather than a hodgepodge of unrelated rules and "tricks."

Build on the foundation you have worked so hard to lay. Not only will it make the new learning easier, but it will also strengthen the underlying principles (Principle of Proportionality and Multiplication Property of Equality) when students see more applications for them.

Several strands from previous lessons reappear in this lesson and are extended to include percents:

- Fraction, decimal, and percent equivalents
- When used with fractions or percents, *of* means "times"
- Solving proportions
- Solving equations that indicate multiplication

Lesson Recommendations

PAGE 226

Mental Math

The purpose of these exercises is to prepare students for the next step of connecting fractions, decimals, and percents.

Getting Comfortable with Percents

This introduction to percents is an intuitive approach that is intended to leave students with a broad overview of the concept. It is also intended to show students that many of the most often-used percents can be dealt with conceptually and without formal algorithms. Students should be able to handle these problems mentally after the extensive groundwork laid in the fractions lesson. An additional benefit of these pages is that students will be left with certain benchmarks by which they can judge the reasonableness of answers in more complicated problems.

Be sure to establish the mental benchmarks before students get caught up in rules and procedures. The benchmarks help students to generate a big picture of what percent means and how the numbers involved are related.

The problems below can also help students to establish the big picture of percents. In the first set, all the numbers in a percent relation are given, and students are asked to organize them in the "percent sentence."

(___ is ___% of ___) or (___% of ___ is ___)

For problems 1–6 use the numbers given to make true percent sentences. Do not use a calculator or paper and pencil to compute.

1. 7, 14, 50%

2. 32, 16, 50%

3. $\frac{1}{2}$, 50%, $\frac{1}{4}$

4. 7, 25%, 28

5. 64, 25%, 16

6. $\frac{1}{2}$, $\frac{1}{8}$, 25%

Circle the answer that makes the equation true. Again, no calculators!

7. 20 is (50% or 200%) of 40

8. 20 is (50% or 200%) of 10

9. 50% of (88 or 22) is 44

10. 300% of (4, 36) is 12

EXTENSION ACTIVITY

Creating Additional Problems (in pairs)

If your students responded well to **Problem 8** on page 230, you can expand this section by challenging them to devise easy ways to find a percent of a number. For example,

- 26% of a number (by adding 25% and 1% of it)
- 9% of a number (by subtracting 1% from 10% of it)
- 92% of a number (by subtracting 10% of it and then adding 1% of it twice)

A colleague from the Netherlands, Mieke van Groenestijn, writes of adult students who have refined this benchmark method (using various combinations of easy percents) to the point where it is the only method that they use to solve percent problems.

Compliment your students' progress in gaining confidence in their mental skills. Stress the value of their mental skills in their daily lives and encourage them to keep practicing whenever they can.

PAGES 231–235

Percent Equations as Proportions

Two methods or algorithms for solving percent problems are presented. I recommend that you teach both of them, proceeding straight through the pages in the order given. Students who can use both methods can choose between them to fit the situation that is presented. Each has some advantages over the other. The proportion method is often easier for students to learn and remember, but it is not as easy to apply to more complex situations like percent change. The algebraic equation method allows an easy transition to using the % key on the calculator.

Both methods begin with the **percent equation**. Students must be able to distill the information from a word problem into the template of this equation before they proceed to find the answer by either method. Most of the difficulties arise from students trying to decide which of the numbers is the *amount* and which is the *base*. The big picture work that we have already done in this lesson will be helpful, but you can also help by instructing them to focus on the base. Teach them to ask, "percent *of* what?"

At this stage in their study, students should have made significant gains in their ability to reason abstractly with symbols. Solving a percent equation directly for any one of the missing variables should be fairly easy by now. For those who still struggle, a reminder of the triangle that pictures a multiplicative relationship (page 91) may help. Label it with the words from the percent equation.

PERCENT RELATIONSHIP

Using the % key on the calculator follows the logic of the algebraic method where the variable is isolated on its side of the equation before the problem is entered into the calculator.

EXTENSION ACTIVITY

Percent or Dollars Off?   (small groups and whole class)

This problem should promote a discussion that calls attention to the importance of the *base* in percent problems. You can use it either at the beginning of class or at the end, wherever it will generate the most discussion. It represents the kind of question that asks students to think for themselves rather than to depend on established rules.

Which Would You Choose? $10 OFF   or   10% OFF

If a student's answer to the question is "It depends," he or she already understands an important aspect of working with percent. Percent is a rate that means "out of a hundred," but it does not exist by itself; percent is always "of" something. To answer the question above, consider the base of the percent. Ask students these three questions:

When does 10% equal $10?   (Only when the price of an item is exactly $100.)

When is 10% less than $10?   (When the item costs less than $100.)

When is 10% more than $10?   (When the price is more than $100.)

PAGE 236

Using Data

Students will not be asked the details of circle graph or pie chart construction on the GED Test, but this activity will deepen their understanding of the basis for the structure of such charts. From the start, you should emphasize that the entire circle represents 100% of the people surveyed. To reinforce this idea, ask students to add the percentages in the table. The central angle is the feature that is used to determine the boundaries of the wedges in the chart. The size of the central angle in each wedge is found by finding the percentages of 360°.

You can use this activity to show students how to use a protractor in drawing angles, or you can choose to merely estimate the size of the wedges. Estimation will work quite well for this set of values because two of the wedges represent 25%; their central angles will measure 90°, a simple angle to estimate.

If you choose to estimate the angle sizes, instruct the students to draw the two right angles first in the top half of the circle. Then use proportional reasoning to determine the remaining boundary. The portion that is remaining is 20% of the circle and must be divided into portions that are 15% and 5%. Students might choose to make marks on the circumference that divide the portion into fourths and then allot $\frac{3}{4}$ to 15% and $\frac{1}{4}$ to 5%.

When a circle graph is accurately drawn, each feature of a circle, the circumference, the area, as well as the central angle, is divided according to the percentages given in the table.

PAGE 237

More Applications

Problems 13 and **14** give practice in finding percentages, but a comparison of the two will highlight the importance of considering the base of a percent before making judgments. To facilitate the comparison, ask students to label the answers they are finding in both questions as they proceed. These are actual situations from a newspaper, so they involve messier numbers and more complex questions than the students are used to. If necessary, guide the class through the steps of the problems so that the point about the importance of the base can be made.

To solidify the idea, ask questions like these:

- A group of employees agreed to a 10% reduction in salary to help a company through a fiscal crisis. Later, they were given a 10% raise. Were their final salaries equal to their original ones? If not, which was greater? (Original salaries would be greater because 10% of the lowered salary would not be as much as the reduction.)

- A store raised prices on all merchandise by 10% on July 15. August 15 was the first day of a "Back to School Sale" where the prices on all merchandise were lowered by 10%. Compare the price of an item on July 14 to its price on August 16. Are the prices the same? If not, which price is less? (The sale price on August 16 is less than the price on July 14 because 10% of the raised price would be greater than 10% of the original price.)

OBJECTIVES

Students will be able to

- use benchmark percents to estimate when finding percentages and rates
- find simple interest and determine the rate of interest charged
- recognize percent change as a description that relates actual change to the original value
- solve percent increase/decrease problems

Background

Working with Percents

This lesson, like the first percent lesson, contains some intuitive and conceptual work as well as the more formal work on percent of increase and decrease. References are made to both methods of solution (using proportions and using equations) but the reasoning that sets up the techniques for finding percent increase and decrease is based on the algebraic equation.

Lesson Recommendations

PAGES 242–244

Mental Math

The purpose of these exercises is to remind students of the link between fractions and percents in the benchmarks from the preceding lesson.

Estimating Using Benchmark Percents

This section extends the mental work of the last lesson. Students can estimate only if they know the benchmark percents and fractions established in the last lesson. Finding compatible numbers for division is again the key element when estimating. Students may need a brief review of compatible numbers before you begin.

While completing **Problem 1**, ask students to indicate whether each actual answer will be greater or less than the estimate before they find the actual answers with the calculator.

It is important to take the time to talk about how valuable these estimation skills are in everyday situations. For example, talk about estimating before going to pay the cashier. A person who can estimate is never surprised at the amount that comes up on the cash register.

Tipping is perhaps the most common situation where estimating is good enough to determine the amount to leave.

When finding the rate of percent by either method, one always divides the *amount* by the *base*, a problem that can be expressed in fraction form. By rounding the numbers so that the fraction can be easily reduced, estimating the rate becomes a familiar problem to your students.

PAGES 244–245

Simple Interest

Point out to students that the way simple interest is computed in this section is really not the way most interest is computed in today's society. With the aid of computers, banks pay **compound interest** (interest on the principle and on the interest earned to date). However, the basic idea of paying for the use of money is introduced here.

Fractional and decimal percents also are introduced in the context in which they most often occur.

PAGES 245–246

Change

This small section introduces percent change as a description of change that takes the size of the original number into consideration. That is, it tells how the amount of change is related to the size of the original amount. To understand the full impact of change, one usually would like to know both the percent change (relative change) and the actual change.

EXTENSION ACTIVITY

Where Did the Rate Change the Most? (small groups)

In the first column of page 294 in the Appendix, the graphs show the change from 1990 to 2000 in the percentage of homes that fall into the different price ranges. Since the number of houses has likely changed over the decade, the same percentage in 1990 does not mean the same number of houses as it does in 2000. Thus, when applied to these data, *actual change* refers to the difference between the percentages from 1990 to 2000. Be sure that you are consistent in the vocabulary that you use. *Actual change* can be called the "change in percentages" or "difference in percentages" and *relative change* can be called "percent change."

At this point in the course, I would not clarify the terms before I ask the first question. I would hope that at least one of the groups would make the expected error and provide a great learning opportunity for all.

1. *With respect to actual change, rank the four categories from greatest to least. Show the result of your calculations.*

   (Actual change can be visualized by how much difference (subtract) there is between the lengths of the two bars. **1.** Less than $99,000, difference is 23%; **2.** $100,000 – $199,000, difference is 14%; **3.** $200,000 – $499,000, difference is 7%; **4.** $500,000 or more, difference is 1%.)

2. *With respect to relative change, rank the four categories from greatest to least. Show the result of your calculations.*

(Relative change is the actual change divided by the original number.
1. $200,000 – $499,000, $\frac{7}{11} = 64\%$; **2.** $100,000 – $199,000, $\frac{14}{24} = 58\%$; **3.** $500,000 or more, $\frac{1}{2} = 50\%$; **4.** Less than $99,000, $\frac{23}{63} = 36.5\%$.)

3. *Which price range showed the greatest change?*

(When asked in these words, the answer could be either one of the two that are ranked number one. How should the question be asked if you wanted the answer to be "less than $99,000"?)

4. *Which of the following statements would be accurate interpretations of the data?*

■ *The price of homes that are over $500,000 went up by 50% in the decade.* (F)

■ *The number of homes that are over $500,000 went up by 50% in the decade.* (F)

■ *The percentage of homes that are over $500,000 went up by 50% in the decade.* (T)

5. *Tell whether or not each statement is supported by the data.*

■ *In 2000 21% of the homes in the U.S. were valued at over $200,000.* (T)

■ *In 1990 nearly 90% of the homes in the U.S. were valued at less than $200,000.* (T)

■ *In 2000 the ratio between the number of homes over $500,000 and the number of homes between $200,000 and $499,000 is 1 to 6.* (T)

PAGES 246–247

Percent Decrease

Discounts on merchandise and automobile depreciation provide the real-life applications for the problems in this section. Two methods are shown to find the discounted price, and students are asked to find it in both ways so that they recognize their equivalence.

The diagram clearly shows the relationship between the percentages as relative descriptions and the dollars as the actual numbers. For this case, the original price of $150 is separated into two parts, $105 and $45. The diagram shows that, relatively speaking, this is equivalent to 100% being separated into 70% and 30%.

PAGE 248

Percent Increase

The two methods are again shown for finding the value after an increase. Compare the diagram in this example with the one for percent decrease. Point out that in both cases the original number (the base of the percent) is shaded and in both cases the shaded part represents 100%. Whether it is a decrease or an increase determines whether the actual change and % change are subtracted or added to this base.

EXTENSION ACTIVITY

Stressing the Base of Percent (individual and in pairs)

Use this activity as a quick in-class assessment to see whether or not your students have learned the importance of focusing on the base of the percent. You may need to review the terms that are used.

Copy the following problem situation on the board, excluding the answers given in parentheses. Instruct students (individually) to think about each part of the problem and then discuss each part in pairs. Then fill in the blanks as a class.

A jeweler sells some items at twice the price he paid for them.

selling price = _____% of wholesale price (200%)

profit = _____% of wholesale price (100%)

wholesale price = _____% of selling price (50%)

profit = _____% of selling price (50%)

PAGE 249

Calculator Exploration

The real power of the % key on the calculator surfaces when finding the new amount after a change. The fact that the designers of the calculator chose this to be a single-key operation is indicative of how frequently the problem arises in everyday experience.

Notice that the order of entry is important for this multistep procedure. You must enter the original number first, multiplied by the percent.

PAGES 250–251

Finding the Rate of Increase and Decrease

If necessary, spend time making the connection to the proportional and algebraic equation solving methods from which the ratio, $\frac{\text{amount of increase or decrease}}{\text{original number}}$, is derived. It is important that students be able to reconstruct it if they forget how to find the rate. However, do not demand that students repeat that connection with every problem that they do. Students will be showing intuition about percentages when they begin these problems immediately with a ratio that has the base as its denominator.

The topic of change is explored further by examining two graphs that picture data that are very relevant to the students in your class. The first refers to trend data in the Appendix about GED candidates and the credentials issued in recent years. A second graph describes change in the number of teens who smoke from the Youth Risk Behavior Study. To explore other topics in the survey that may engage your younger students, such as alcohol related behavior, seat belt usage, and sexual behavior, see the Centers for Disease Control and Prevention Website.

Relating Rates and Slopes to Graphs

OBJECTIVES

Students will

- find the slope of a line on a grid graphically or by using the slope formula
- connect the ideas of rate and slope of a line for informational graphs
- connect the features of verbal, symbolic, graphical, and numerical representations of a linear function to one another

Background

Students have seen the fundamental link between rates and slopes of graphs earlier in the book. This lesson formalizes that link by using the coordinate grid and the idea of a linear function.

This lesson starts with the definition students already know: slope $= \frac{\text{rise}}{\text{run}}$. Because the lines are drawn on a grid, students can determine the number of units in the rise and the run, first by counting the squares on a grid and then by subtracting the x- and y-values of points on a graph. Finding a slope is given a context in an informational graph where the slope of a line is the annual increase in expenditures. The slope is a *rate*, dollars per year.

When generalized to algebraic functions, the slope of a line illustrates the *rate* at which one variable changes with respect to the other variable. For example, on a graph of $d = rt$, the slope of the line represents the *rate* of speed (how fast distance changes with respect to time).

An extensive discussion of a craftsperson's financial considerations provides the context for an examination of linear functions. The verbal descriptions of the situations are translated to tables, equations, and graphs so students can see the real-life significance of the features of slope and y-intercept. If students follow the story carefully, they should be able to interpret these features in graphs of other situations.

Lesson Recommendations

PAGE 254

Mental Math

The purpose of these exercises is to review what students know about integers. Students are then prepared for the application of integers presented in this lesson.

PAGES 254–255

More About Slopes

The slope of a straight line is the same regardless of which two points on the line are chosen to determine the rise and the run. The horizontal and vertical distances between the points change proportionally so the ratios between them can all be simplified to the same one.

You can eliminate some confusion by having students focus on the slope of a line from left to right. With this in mind, if the line leans downward, it has a negative slope. If the line leans upward, it has a positive slope. Remind students to check the reasonableness of their answers by asking which way, up or down, the line is leaning. A horizontal line has a slope of 0. And finally, a vertical line has an undefined slope because 0 is the denominator. (Never divide by 0.)

PAGES 256–257

Finding Slopes from Coordinates

The formula for finding slopes from the coordinates (x, y) is introduced here. Students are often intimidated when they first see the formula from the Formulas page. The examples and problems on these two pages are structured to show that the formula, while it looks complex, is merely describing the process that students have already been using to find the slope. The formula, by itself, has value in that it allows one to find the slope without plotting the points on a graph.

Take time to explain the subscripts and their purpose in ensuring that the x- and y-values of the two points are subtracted in the same order. It is not important which point is chosen to be point 1 and which is point 2. However, the order of subtraction must remain *consistent* for both the rise and the run.

Do not insist on mastery of the formula without an accompanying graph. Let the picture (points on the graph) help students to understand the procedures that the symbols are describing. In this way, you will remove some of the mystery from mathematical notations in general.

PAGE 258

Slopes from Informational Graphs

When points on a graph are determined from data, the graph is called an informational graph. Students plot the data on a graph in the activity on this page. They find the slope of the straight line and use it to estimate a value between two given points (interpolation) and to predict a value beyond the ones given (extrapolation). This path of reverse reasoning requires more understanding than merely repeating the process of finding slopes.

PAGES 259–261

Graphs of Linear Functions

The story of Elena transforming bottles into cruets and selling them gives an adult context to the algebraic ideas of linear functions. Some groups of your students may be able to progress through the problems on their own, but class discussion of each new question would enhance the learning of these algebraic topics. They may not be topics that you remember from your own algebra training, but they are important topics for the GED Mathematics Test. Do not skip this last section!

The graphs of function are different from the lines in the informational graph in that they represent a mathematical rule. Students first construct a table of values that reflects the verbal description of the situation. That process makes the next step, writing the equation, easier. Finally, students plot the points on a grid and draw the line connecting them, the graph of the function. The graph, the table, and the equation all represent the function.

Focus first on the costs that Elena will incur. The point at which the line intersects the *y*-axis is called the *y*-intercept, but it is more important to emphasize that this is the point (from the table and equation) where the value of *x* is zero. In our story, it is the amount of money she has to spend to be able to start her enterprise. In economics, this is called the *fixed cost* but can also be thought of as *up-front costs* or *start-up costs*.

The slope is found from the graph and then related to the story and the equation. Again it represents the rate, in this case, the cost per bottle.

Every linear function can be expressed using an equation in the format, $y = mx + b$. The two features we have discussed, *y*-intercept and slope, can be read directly from the equation. The value of the constant term (no variable involved), *b*, is the *y*-value of the *y*-intercept; and the value of the coefficient of *x*, *m* (the number that is multiplied by *x*), is the slope.

$$\underset{\text{y-intercept}}{y = \overset{\overset{\text{slope}}{\downarrow}}{m}x + \underset{\uparrow}{b}}$$

Problems 11 and **12** construct hypothetical situations and ask students to repeat the process of finding the equation, completing a table, and plotting the points on the graph. Students should draw the new lines on the same axis as the previous one so that comparing them will be easy. In **Problem 11**, one feature, the unit rate, is changed. The one feature of the equation that is changed is the coefficient of *x* and the one changed feature of the resulting graph is the slope. Similarly, in **Problem 12**, the one feature that is changed is the fixed cost. As a result, *b* changes in the equation and the *y*-intercept changes on the graph.

Problem 13 asks students to generalize these findings to context-free equations.

When Elena sells the cruets, she generates revenue. Students will graph the revenue line on the coordinate grid where the cost line is already shown. This adds interest to the graph in that there is a point where the two lines intersect, the break-even point. The *x*-value of this point represents the number of cruets she must sell to recover her costs. **Problems 15** and **16** ask students to estimate values from the graph and validate their estimates by using the equations.

GED Practice Test

OBJECTIVES

Students will

- diagnose their own areas of weakness and complete the necessary review before attempting the actual GED Test
- develop confidence about their success on the test

Lesson Recommendations

PAGES 264–266

Test-Taking Tips

The first tips are reminders of some of the most important math-related tips given earlier in the student book. Then some general test-taking tips are discussed. I have spoken to teachers who assert that the GED Mathematics Test is really a reading test. In many respects, that is true. Examinees must be able to understand how to interpret the quantitative information from the verbal descriptions of the situations. Thus, "Read the Problems Carefully" is the most important tip to leave with your students before they take the test.

After students experience the time allowed for the practice test that follows, they will have an idea about how to pace themselves for the actual test. Most students will have time to reread each question to verify that they understood it correctly the first time. For the tough questions, advise them to use analytical reading techniques, such as figuring out the meaning of unfamiliar words from the context and from the words that they know, deciding which words are the critical ones to the question, and paraphrasing the question in their own words.

Throughout the book, students have used copies of the actual test enclosures that give directions for filling in the alternate format answer grids and for using the Casio *fx*-260 calculator. They also have been using the Formulas page as a reference. Students have a sense of what is on these pages but should be advised to refer to them whenever it is appropriate for an item on the test.

Finally, as a last resort, I provide one of the standard tips for multiple-choice test takers: try each of the alternatives and see which answer works.

PAGES 266–277

GED Practice Test

If you administer the practice test under the same guidelines as the actual test, students can become familiar with the constraints. Since students have seen this test in the back of their book throughout the course, it cannot serve as a reliable predictor of their success on the actual test. Moreover, although the problems have been chosen so that they represent the content and cognitive aspects of an actual test, they have not undergone the stringent review process that items on an actual test have. Nevertheless, it can serve as a valuable diagnostic tool, review organizer, and confidence builder. As an accurate predictor of success, use the Official GED Practice Tests for those students you feel are ready.

After all the tests have been graded, analyze the results. For your class review time, focus on the test items that about half your students missed. This tactic will be more effective than discussing all 50 of the items in one session.

Ask students to share their problem-solving strategies with others. By reminding them that the method of solution in the back of the student book is only one way to solve a problem, encourage students to be inventive in their approach to problems. You want to bring out the nonacademic, nonalgorithmic, common sense reasons for why they chose the right answers. When students compare their strategies, some will gain more insight, and most will gain confidence.

Your intuition may tell you to start your class review with the problems that all the students missed because these are areas of real trouble. However, these problems may be the kinds that need extended discussion that only a few can follow. Now is not the time to confuse students with the more obscure topics. On an individual basis, encourage students to ask for explanations of other problems that they still don't understand.

Students who are scheduled to take the actual test will likely confide that they are feeling test anxiety. Everyone experiences it to some degree, and there are many personal remedies. Some students say that a cup of coffee will allow them to think faster. Others say that they get "wired" by coffee and can't think systematically. Personally, I find that nothing is as effective as the relaxing effect that confidence brings. This is why the least difficult items tend to be at the beginning of the GED Test. Success breeds success. Encourage students to skip problems that seem difficult to them and return to those problems later after they have loosened up their thinking processes with easier problems.

Post-GED

The statistics on page 284 of the Appendix report that 65.5% of GED candidates have said that they are planning further study. In terms of mathematics, your successful students are ready for a basic algebra course as offered by many community colleges. Encourage them to take the next step in self-improvement and enroll in a class. Suggest instructors who have a reputation for making the subject accessible to all learners.

Analysis of Selected Items from the GED Practice Test

Reading each word of the problem carefully is especially important in **Problem 7**. It says, "10% off the *current* price" which means that the base of the percent changes with each deduction.

The graph on long distance price plans provides the stimulus for **Problems 9–12**. In **Problem 9**, students need to recognize that the question is asking for the cost when the number of minutes is zero—the *y*-intercept. For **Problem 11**, the intersection point of the line for Plan A and the line for Plan B gives a value of 33 for the minutes. In **Problem 12**, students must look for the *horizontal* distance between Plan A and Plan C to find the difference in minutes.

Problem 17 could be done in a number of ways. By substituting 3 for the variable *x* in the equation, the result is $y = \frac{1}{3}(3) - 4$ or $1 - 4 = -3$. Of course, some may have used the slope, counting up 1 and over 3 until they got to a point where *x* was 3.

In **Problem 20**, students needed to see that the central angle of the wedge that is bounded by arc *BD* is $\frac{1}{8}$ of the circle. Thus, the arc will be $\frac{1}{8}$ of the circumference.

For **Problems 23–25**, students could use either or both the chart and the graph.

Problem 34 asks students to choose an equation from examining the values in the table. This was the topic of the last lesson, but some may have just substituted the values in each equation to figure it out.

Problem 37 represents an unfamiliar topic to most students. They should see that point *F* is 4 units directly above point *D*. Since the shape of the figure does not change as it is moved, point *F* will still be 4 units directly above point *D* when it is at $(-3, -5)$.

The graph for **Problem 46** uses BMI>30 as the definition of obesity. It is a difficult graph to read, requiring careful attention to the legends. The data from which this graph is drawn is in the last two columns in the table on page 287 of the Appendix. If you have time, study the data in the second column that says (essentially) that over half of the U.S. citizens are overweight or obese. This data has prompted many newspaper and magazine articles and has even caused the government to make changes to their traditional food pyramid. A point to discuss in this regard is the definition of overweight in the BMI chart on the preceding page. Many view it as being too rigorous, especially for men.

If a student finds the answer to **Problem 50** as suggested on the answer page, he or she will be estimating within an algebraic procedure, which most will not think to do. But the test tips from the beginning of the lesson can be illustrated with this item. First of all, students should get the formula for the area of a circle from the Formulas page. After recognizing that the rotating arm is the radius of the circle and remembering that the value of π is a little more than 3, students can substitute the given values into the area formula $(A = \pi r^2)$ to find that $r = 10$ gives an area of about 300 square feet.

BASIC FACTS

+	0	1	2	3	4	5	6	7	8	9
0	0	1	2	3	4	5	6	7	8	9
1	1	2	3	4	5	6	7	8	9	10
2	2	3	4	5	6	7	8	9	10	11
3	3	4	5	6	7	8	9	10	11	12
4	4	5	6	7	8	9	10	11	12	13
5	5	6	7	8	9	10	11	12	13	14
6	6	7	8	9	10	11	12	13	14	15
7	7	8	9	10	11	12	13	14	15	16
8	8	9	10	11	12	13	14	15	16	17
9	9	10	11	12	13	14	15	16	17	18

×	0	1	2	3	4	5	6	7	8	9
0	0	0	0	0	0	0	0	0	0	0
1	0	1	2	3	4	5	6	7	8	9
2	0	2	4	6	8	10	12	14	16	18
3	0	3	6	9	12	15	18	21	24	27
4	0	4	8	12	16	20	24	28	32	36
5	0	5	10	15	20	25	30	35	40	45
6	0	6	12	18	24	30	36	42	48	54
7	0	7	14	21	28	35	42	49	56	63
8	0	8	16	24	32	40	48	56	64	72
9	0	9	18	27	36	45	54	63	72	81

1	2	3	4	5	6	7	8	9	10
11	12	13	14	15	16	17	18	19	20
21	22	23	24	25	26	27	28	29	30
31	32	33	34	35	36	37	38	39	40
41	42	43	44	45	46	47	48	49	50
51	52	53	54	55	56	57	58	59	60
61	62	63	64	65	66	67	68	69	70
71	72	73	74	75	76	77	78	79	80
81	82	83	84	85	86	87	88	89	90
91	92	93	94	95	96	97	98	99	100

NUMBER LINES

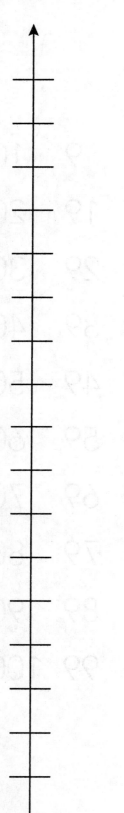

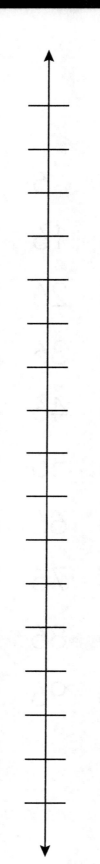

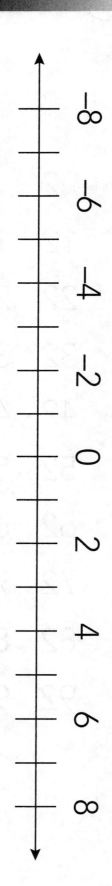

PLACE-VALUE CHART

trillions	10^{12}	,
hundred billions	10^{11}	
ten billions	10^{10}	
billions	10^{9}	,
hundred millions	10^{8}	
ten millions	10^{7}	
millions	10^{6}	,
hundred thousands	10^{5}	
ten thousands	10^{4}	
thousands	10^{3}	,
hundreds	10^{2}	
tens	10^{1}	
ones	10^{0}	
tenths	10^{-1}	• ← decimal point
hundredths	10^{-2}	
thousandths	10^{-3}	

113

R U L E R S

These rulers have been enlarged for ease of use.

FRACTION TABLE

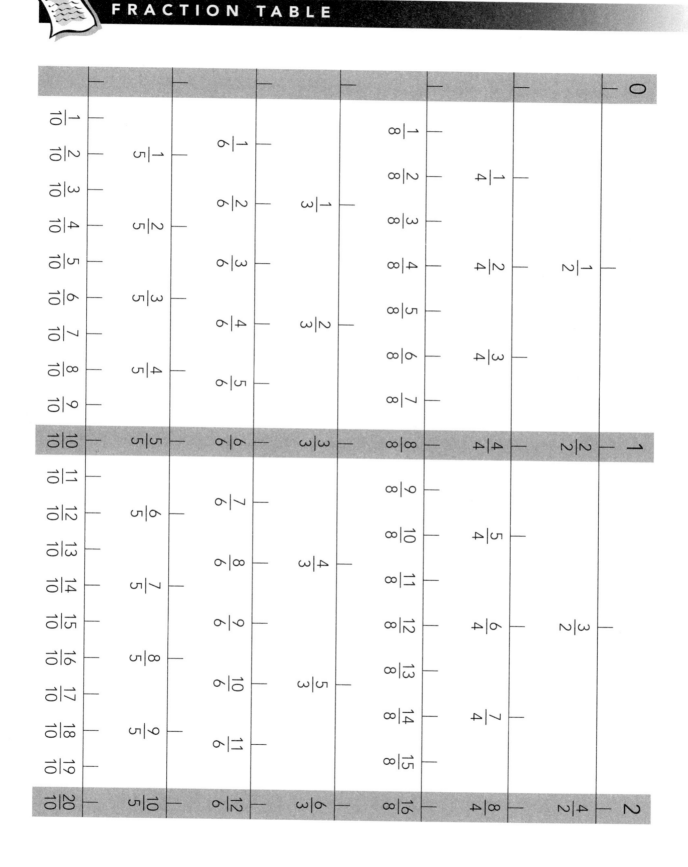

TENTHS/HUNDRETHS GRIDS

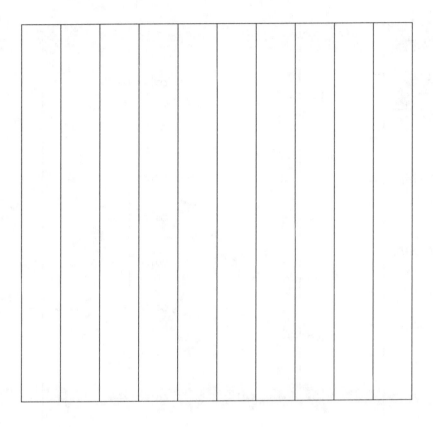

CENTIMETER GRID

POLYGONS

Directions: Cut on all solid lines.